INCREDIBLE QUESTS:

EPIC JOURNEYS IN MYTH & LEGEND

PHILIP STEELE

Illustrations by Sue Climpson

southwater

This edition is published by Southwater

Southwater is an imprint of Anness Publishing Ltd
Hermes House, 88–89 Blackfriars Road, London SE1 8HA
tel. 020 7401 2077; fax 020 7633 9499
www.southwaterbooks.com; info@anness.com

© Anness Publishing Ltd 2003, 2006

UK agent: The Manning Partnership Ltd,
6 The Old Dairy, Melcombe Road,
Bath BA2 3LR; tel. 01225 478444; fax 01225 478440;
sales@manning-partnership.co.uk

UK distributor: Grantham Book Services Ltd, Isaac Newton Way,
Alma Park Industrial Estate, Grantham, Lincs NG31 9SD;
tel. 01476 541080; fax 01476 541061; orders@gbs.tbs-ltd.co.uk

North American agent/distributor: National Book Network,
4501 Forbes Boulevard, Suite 200, Lanham, MD 20706;
tel. 301 459 3366; fax 301 429 5746; www.nbnbooks.com

Australian agent/distributor: Pan Macmillan Australia, Level 18,
St Martins Tower, 31 Market St, Sydney, NSW 2000;
tel. 1300 135 113; fax 1300 135 103; customer.service@macmillan.com.au

New Zealand agent/distributor: David Bateman Ltd,
30 Tarndale Grove, Off Bush Road, Albany, Auckland;
tel. (09) 415 7664; fax (09) 415 8892

Publisher: Joanna Lorenz
Managing Editor: Linda Fraser
Editor: Joy Wotton
Editorial Reader: Penelope Goodare
Consultant Editor: Gilly Cameron Cooper
Consultant: Michael Jordan
Designer: Sarah Williams
Map Artwork: David Cook
Picture Research: Su Alexander
Copy Editor: Tracey Kelly

Previously published as *Myths and Legends from
Around the World: Incredible Journeys*

10 9 8 7 6 5 4 3 2 1

Picture credits
b=bottom
The Publishers wish to thank the following
for permission to reproduce illustrations.
Peter Newark's American Pictures: 9b. Mary Evans
Picture Library: 13b. Cadw: 14b. Ancient Art and
Architecture Collection: 20b, 31b, 32b, /Charles Tait:
16b, /Cheryl Hogue: 19b, /G. Tortol: 22b, 36b, /B.
Norman: 26b, /Ronald Sheridan: 40b. Robert Harding
Picture Library: 42b.

Contents

Travelers' Tales

The stories in this book come from all over the world, from many different ages. Some were probably first told around campfires in the Stone Age, and others were recited in Roman palaces, on Viking longships, and in the halls of medieval castles. All of them are living stories, still told today—in books, comic strips, television, films, and even computer games. Each generation gains something from the tales before passing them down to the next generation.

Although these myths and legends began in many different lands, they have in common a sense of wonder for human life and experiences, a respect for the natural world, a love of adventure, and a sense of humor.

Myths and legends attempt to explain natural phenomena, such as volcanoes, earthquakes, whirlwinds, floods, and other disasters. These are often represented as powerful gods. Volcanoes are named after the Roman god of fire, Vulcan.

What are myths?

Myths are ancient tales that try to answer the big questions. Where did life come from? What happens to us when we die? Why does the sun cross the sky? Myths tell stories about our most basic hopes and fears. Macsen's dream shows how powerful love is, and King Gilgamesh is obsessed by death after his best friend dies. Although they are about human men, women, and children, myths also tell of gods and goddesses, spirits and demons.

What are legends?

Legends are also ancient tales, but unlike myths, these are stories about heroes, heroines, and villains. Many legends are based on stories about historical figures, real wars, and natural disasters such as floods. Many of them became what are known as "epics"—long poems telling

On their Journey to the West, Monkey, Brother Tripitaka, and their companions Greedy Pig and Sandy, the water monster, met the Buddha himself. Their story, like many ancient legends, is a cheerful mixture of fables, fairy tales, legends, and religious beliefs.

The search for the Holy Grail became a part of the legend of the British warrior king, Arthur, and his knights of the Round Table.

stories of heroic events and characters who make a long journey filled with challenges. As stories are told and told again, historical facts become confused and deeds become exaggerated, until the legend takes on a life of its own. The original myths and legends often become intertwined with later religious beliefs.

One example is the case of the legendary King Arthur. He was probably a Celtic warrior who fought against the Saxons in Britain almost 1,500 years ago. Storytellers praised his deeds, and they added all sorts of mythical details to his character, which had once been told about an ancient Celtic god called Bran. In addition, over the next 600 years or so, Christian elements were brought into the story, so that Arthur's knights rode in search of the Holy Grail.

Another story in this book tells of a Chinese supernatural hero called Monkey. Tales about this colorful character are drawn from three different religions, and they include a mixture of history, proverbs, superstitions, and ancient beliefs about magic and the spirit world.

Journeys and voyages

Many of these tales are about journeys over land or sea, and people even told stories about flights through air and space (long before it was actually possible for them to do some of these things). They explain how humans traveled to the world of the gods, or how gods and goddesses came down to Earth. Other epic stories describe journeys to spirit worlds and lands of the dead, for people regarded death as a journey, always wondering if it was possible to return from the land of the dead.

The quest

One special type of traveling tale is called a "quest." In this kind of story, the hero or heroine has to set out on a journey during which he or she is given a series of challenges, often by a god or goddess. The hero has to succeed in each task in order to prove his value, either in spiritual or practical terms. The West African hero Kwaku Ananse, for instance, has to prove to the sky god that he is cunning and resourceful enough to be a spinner of tales.

Some stories try to explain what happens after death. Aeneas, the Trojan hero, visited the underworld to ask his father's ghost for advice.

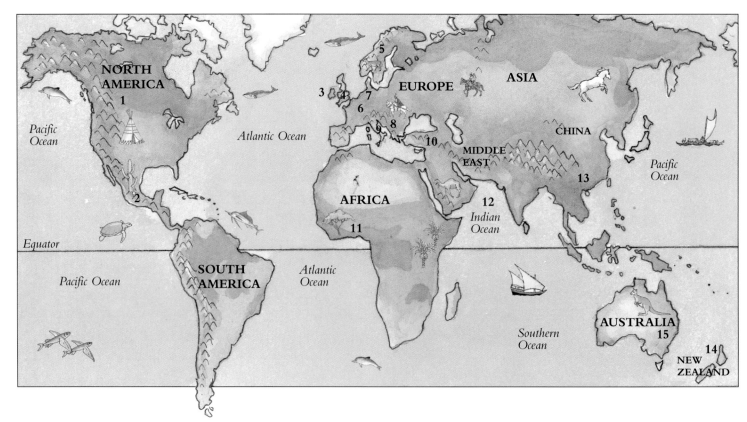

In search of a home

Stories often try to explain how a people first came to the land in which they now live, and why it belongs to them. The *Aeneid* tells the story of how the Romans may have originally come to Italy from ancient Troy, and the legend of Kupe tells how the Maoris traveled from a magical island and discovered New Zealand. One tale explains that the Aztec people had to wander through the wilderness for a number of years eating snakes, before they were told by their god where to build a city.

Myths from around the world

The map shows where the stories in this book come from.
1. Scarface Visits the Sun (North America)
2. The Eagle and the Cactus (Mexico)
3. Oisin and the Land of Youth (Ireland)
4. The Dream of Macsen (Wales)
5. Thor's Journey to Utgard (Scandinavia)
6. Quest for the Holy Grail (Western Europe)
7. The Journey of Doom (Germany)
8. The Wandering Odysseus (Greece)
9. From Troy to Rome (Rome)
10. The King Who Could Not Conquer Death (Babylon)
11. Travels of a Trickster (West Africa)
12. The Seven Voyages of Sindbad (Indian Ocean)
13. The Monkey and the Monk (China)
14. Kupe the Explorer (New Zealand)
15. The One That Got Away (Australia)

Tales of adventure

One of the earliest reasons that people traveled was to trade goods between different countries and territories. Sailors and merchants have always loved to tell tall stories about their voyages and adventures while transporting goods from one land to another, and the stories change as they are passed down to younger generations. People have always enjoyed adventure stories about exotic places, bizarre animals, desert islands, and

Myths are often about spiritual journeys to temples and other sacred sites. Monkey went to India to find the Buddhist scriptures.

Some ancient legends, like the stories about the character of Sindbad, the Sailor, told of exciting adventures in foreign countries.

cannibals, and each time these stories are retold, they may be added to in a different way. The medieval legends about Sindbad the Sailor date back to an age when Arab ships made long and dangerous journeys, and sailed from the Gulf to India, Sri Lanka, China, Indonesia, and East Africa.

Marching off to war

Many of these tales of incredible journeys are about weapons and warriors, for a common reason why ordinary people traveled was to work as soldiers and mercenaries, in the invasion and conquest of other lands. Legends are often brutal and bloodthirsty in their description of combat, but hand-to-hand fighting was something that everyone knew about. In the old stories, fighting may be glorified, but it is also often viewed as terrifying and awesome—as in the feeling of dreadful foreboding that fills the last part of the Germanic tale, Song of the Nibelungs.

Spiritual journeys

Many people travel as part of their faith or religion. In ancient cultures, in countries from Australia to South America, landscapes were sacred, and people traveled across them with a sense of awe. Later, pilgrims traveled to shrines and to holy cities, such as Jerusalem, Mecca, and Varanasi, India. The act of journeying to these places was in itself a form of worship. Other travelers were missionaries and prophets, who traveled the world preaching and teaching, telling people about their beliefs.

Traveling onward

In all the old stories, travel is described as a tough ordeal. People tramp on foot for months and years on end. They ride on camels and horses. They are shipwrecked, captured, and attacked by robbers. Today, we can travel around the world quickly and in great comfort. However, like the heroes of the myths and legends of the past, travel still brings us new experiences.

Journeys tell us about ourselves. They show us other ways of looking at the world. In reading these myths and legends, you can travel around the world, going backward and forward through time, just as if you had a magic carpet at your command.

In many legendary journeys, the hero must cross a raging sea or a stream. This signifies moving from one phase of life to another.

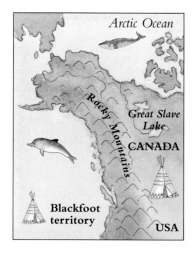

Scarface Visits the Sun

One common reason for an everyday journey is to bring back something useful. Many myths explain human skills and valuable inventions in this way. A human wins or steals a great prize—such as fire—from the gods, and brings it back to Earth. In this traditional tale, a young Native American Blackfoot warrior brings a marvelous secret back from his journey into the sky.

Once there lived a young man, who had an ugly scar on his face. Scarface was a brave warrior, but people thought he looked strange and unlucky.

Ever since he was a boy, Scarface had loved the chief's daughter. She was beautiful, but proud. All the warriors wanted her for a bride, but she turned every one of them away. Scarface, too, declared his love for her, but she dismissed him scornfully. She whispered to her friends about him, and they all laughed unkindly.

The young man felt as if his scar was on fire. He felt angry and miserable, and so he ran and ran until he had left his village far behind. For many days he traveled alone across the land of the wind-blown grass. He saw the thunder clouds and heard the buffalo running, shaking the Earth, but he paid no attention to these things. At last, he collapsed and remembered no more.

Celestial rescue

Morning Star was the son of the Sun and the Moon. He looked down from the heavens and saw the youth lying by a river. "I shall rescue this young man," he told his parents. He came down to Earth and

Morning Star lifted Scarface high up through the clouds to the land of his father, the Sun.

carried the body of the young man named Scarface high into the sky. Scarface awoke and saw the world below, the mountains, the distant forests and wide plains, the silver rivers and shining lakes. At last the two of them reached the hunting grounds of the Sun, who stepped forward and sniffed the human.

"I smell the sickness in him," said Sun. He led him into a place of healing called a sweat lodge, the first that Scarface had ever seen. Sun chanted and burned sweet-smelling grass over the coals. Wreathed in smoke, he passed his healing hands over the human's body. Scarface was then taken through three other sweat lodges. He came out radiant and whole. The livid scar had left his cheeks. Even the Moon now mistook him for her own son. "We shall have to call you 'Mistaken-for-Morning-Star,' " she chuckled.

Morning Star and his new companion rode through the sky-lands each day, and Scarface grew in strength at a rapid pace. One day they were attacked by a flock of screeching birds, with bloody beaks and fierce talons. But Scarface stood his ground bravely, wielding his club to save Morning Star's life.

Sun was overjoyed and began a victory chant that echoed around the sky. He invited Scarface into his tepee and told him a great and magical secret—how to make a sweat lodge, where people could be cleansed and healed. He gave him the sweet-smelling grass and the cleft stick for carrying embers.

"You are now healed," Sun told Scarface. "Take these, journey back to your people, and heal them."

Bringing the gift home

And so Morning Star brought Scarface back to the river bank. Scarface traveled north again across the land. He saw it now with fresh eyes, and seemed to hear the victory song of the Sun everywhere, in the sound of the rushing river and the whistling of the wind. When

When Scarface returned from the Sun, the chief's proud daughter was filled with love for him. In the years that followed, they had many children.

Scarface returned to his people, they did not recognize him. He told them of his journey and how he had been cured. He built for them the first sweat lodge on Earth, and they smelt its sweet smoke. From then on all hurt, pain, and weariness left the village, as if bad spirits had been driven away.

The chief's daughter seemed to shine with a different kind of beauty, now that she realized how cruelly she had treated Scarface before his scar had healed. Soon she grew to love him dearly. Their children and grandchildren never tired of hearing the tale of how Scarface had traveled up to the sky.

CONNECTIONS
• This tale was first told by the Piegans, a people of the Blackfoot, or Siksika, nation. Their homeland is in Montana (now in the United States) and in Saskatchewan (Canada).
• Myths featuring the Sun and Morning Star are believed to have originated in the Southeast, and to have passed to peoples of the Plains, such as the Blackfoot, along trading routes.
• Sweating was used by Native American people to cleanse the body and to cure fevers and aches. The sweat lodge was also believed to purify the spirit before important religious ceremonies and rituals.

Sweat lodges were made of animal skins placed over a wooden frame. Herbs, grasses, and sticks were burned in a sunken pit beneath large stones. Water was poured over the stones when they became hot, so the lodge filled with steam.

The Eagle and the Cactus

At many times in history, whole tribes of people have set off in search of a new home. One such migration was made by the Aztec people through the deserts of Mexico, before they settled at their great capital of Tenochtitlán.

The old man looked at his grandson. "When I was just six years old, just like you," he said, "there was one story I never tired of hearing from the elders. It told how we, the Mexica, had first come to the great city Tenochtitlán. Long, long ago, our people lived on an island in a blue lagoon, far to the northwest. Our home was called Aztlán. Then one day our great leader Huitzilopochtli, whose name means 'Humming-Bird of the South,' called everyone together.

'Arm yourselves with bows, arrows, and nets,' he ordered the men and boys. 'We are setting out on a long, dangerous journey that may

The Culhua hoped that the snakes would kill the Mexica people, but the Mexica simply roasted the snakes and ate them.

take many years.' The women looked worried, and Huitzilopochtli said sternly: 'Fear not, this is the will of the gods. We shall found a great city and conquer the peoples of the world. They will send us tributes of gold, jewelry, and feathers of the quetzal to make fine cloaks.'

So the people of Aztlán packed their bags, gathered their belongings, left their homeland and traveled to Chicomoztoc, the Seven Caves in the Curved Mountain."

A new people

At the Seven Caves of Chicomoztoc, we were reborn as the Mexica, feared by one and all. Huitzilopochtli left this world and was reborn as Lord of the Sun, God of War.

We marched in a long line, like ants, and scratched a living from the desert and ravines, gathering plants and searching for water. We camped in a ruined city and were attacked by the fierce warriors of Azcapotzalco.

We begged the Culhua people for a home. They pretended to be friendly, but the land they gave us was infested with poisonous snakes. They hoped we would die, but instead we roasted the snakes over fires and ate

CONNECTIONS
• This legend is based on historical events. The Aztecs journeyed in search of a new home between about 1100 and 1325. The story later became mixed up with ancient myths.
• The people who ruled Mexico 600 years ago were the Aztecs, "people of Aztlán." They adopted the name "Mexica" during their migration through the deserts of Mexico.
• Today, the modern national flag of Mexico includes the emblem of an eagle landing on a cactus.
• The migration of the Mexica people can be compared with the story of the ancient Hebrews—the "Children of Israel"—who also wandered through the desert in search of a land they could call their own.

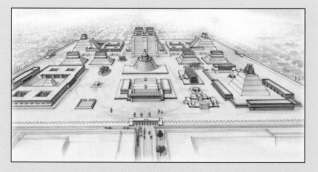

The city of Tenochtitlán, with its vast pyramids, was one of the architectural wonders of the world. The Spaniards destroyed Tenochtitlán during a great battle in 1521. Mexico City was built on the same site. Today, it is one of the biggest cities in the world.

them! We stayed there, and even offered the Culhua our ultimate honor, sacrificing their chief's own daughter to Huitzilopochtli. These ignorant people took this as an insult and chased us away to a lonely, marshy shore.

Had the mighty Huitzilopochtli abandoned his people? In the midst of our misery, he heard our prayers. Our high priest spoke his words: 'I shall give you a sign. Where the eagle lands on the cactus, there shall you build my city.' Eagerly, we waited for dawn to break."

The sign

Early the next morning, our warriors searched the shore. Very soon an excited cry went up, and there on an island in the lake stood a spiny cactus with blood-red flowers. There, too, an eagle was alighting, with sharp talons, pointed beak, and quivering, outstretched wings.

We named this place Tenochtitlán, or 'place of the cactus rock,' and built a shrine to Huitzilopochtli. Today, his shrine sits atop the Great Temple of Tenochtitlán."

When they spotted the eagle landing on a cactus, the Mexica realized they had found their new homeland.

Oisin and the Land of Youth

Irish legends tell of the deeds of Fionn Mac Cumhail, his band of warriors called the Fianna, and his son Oisin, who traveled to a magical land. This story is rooted in ancient Celtic beliefs. In the medieval period, these beliefs were overlaid with Christian values.

Below the mountains and the forest, a chill white mist floated over the still waters of Lough Leane. It shrouded the reeds along the lake shore, where Fionn Mac Cumhail was riding out to hunt deer. Fionn was Ireland's greatest warrior, the leader of the Fianna, a company of heroes. Fionn gazed proudly at his son, Oisin, who was riding alongside the master of the hunt at the head of the Fianna.

Suddenly, Oisin held up his hand in warning. The riders halted and fell silent, one and all. Out of the mist appeared a lovely maiden on a white horse, and she rode along the bank to meet them. Her hair was golden and her cloak was crimson. "Who are you, lady?" challenged the master of the hunt in a hoarse, uncertain voice.

For all his strength, he was shaken by this ghostly vision.

"My name is Niamh Chinn Oir," she replied. "I have come for Oisin."

"I am he," replied Oisin. "From where do you ride?"

"I come from the land of Tir na nÓg, the Land of Youth beyond the western sea," said Niamh. "My father is king. Travel with me to find a land where it is always spring,

Oisin tumbled through time and lost his fairy kingdom in the west.

where the music is sweet and the wine flows freely. There you shall fight no more, but live in a palace with a hundred warriors at your command. I shall be your wife."

A heavy silence hung in the air. The horses fidgeted. At last Fionn muttered, "Fairy magic!" and reached for his sword. But already Oisin's horse was walking into the mist.

Riding over the waves

Niamh galloped through the parting mist, over rolling hills and silver sands, and at last into the green, salty sea. Oisin followed her, enchanted. The horses' hooves skimmed the white foam as they rose into the air. They rode on and on into an ever brighter haze, which shimmered with rainbows. The ocean stretched in all directions. There was no sign of solid land, and yet they rode past soaring towers of glass. They passed a deer being chased through the clouds by a white hound with red ears. They passed a girl on a horse, carrying a golden apple, pursued by a noble youth.

Magical wedding

The journey took an age—or was it a moment? They never stopped to eat or rest, but Oisin felt no hunger. At last their horses' hoofs thudded across solid green turf. Oisin looked around in amazement. The land of Tir na nÓg was sunny, with meadows, fruit trees, and clear, flowing streams. Oisin wedded Niamh and everything in the land of Tir na nÓg was as wonderful as promised. The palace, the hunting, the banquets, and the laughter seemed to be beyond all human happiness.

After three years, Oisin decided to pay a visit to his father and his comrades in the Fianna. "Go back to see them," wept Niamh, "but do not dismount. If you set foot on Irish soil, you will never return to Tir na nÓg."

Oisin galloped over the crests of the swelling waves as he followed Niamh into a swirling mist.

A chilling change

Oisin saddled his horse and journeyed back across the waves until he saw the hills of Ireland rise from the horizon. As he rode through the land of his childhood and youth, it seemed to him that things were smaller than he remembered. The people seemed frail and careworn. Where was his father's stronghold? The hilltop was empty and bare. And where were the baying hounds and cries of the Fianna? The woods were silent.

Oisin saw some villagers heaving at a boulder, and leaned from his saddle to lend a hand. He slipped and fell to the ground. His fine clothes turned to rags. His sword became a stick. His hair turned white. He bellowed in astonishment, but the cracked voice of an old man piped forth. "Where is Fionn, my father?" he cried. "He shall undo this spell."

"Fionn Mac Cumhail?" replied the villagers, suddenly afraid. "Fionn has been dead for 300 years!"

"And my bold companions of the Fianna?"

"Their skeletons lie in the frozen earth."

Oisin realized each year in Tir na nÓg had lasted a hundred in the mortal world. He had paid dearly for following Niamh to the land of eternal youth.

Back in Ireland, the age of gods and magic had passed. Christian monks cared for Oisin through his dying days, but they never understood why his eyes always turned west, across the sea, searching for a distant land.

CONNECTIONS
• Fionn Mac Cumhail may have been an Irish ruler about 2,200 years ago. He was a brave and powerful warrior.
• Many Celtic myths refer to a magical land. The Irish called it Tir na nÓg ("land of the young ones"), or Tir inna mBéo ("land of the living ones"). The Welsh called it Ynys Afallon (the Isle of Avalon), and believed that this magical land was the final resting place of King Arthur.

Many ancient Celtic myths tell of distant lands of immortality, among western lakes or oceans, beneath the setting sun.

The Dream of Macsen

The legend of Macsen is found in the Mabinogion, a series of tales that were written down in Wales during the Middle Ages. Most of these tales are about ancient magic and gods. The story of Emperor Macsen and his journey north to find Elen, however, is different. Probably based on history, it dates from when the Romans occupied Britain. The historical characters became mixed up as the story was passed from one generation to the next.

The emperor Macsen went out hunting in the hills near Rome. In the midday heat, he tired of the chase and dismounted. He left his companions and wandered into a cool, shady grove. There he sat on a mossy bank and

Macsen lay under a shady tree, dreaming of a splendid palace.

drank from a cold, fresh stream. He lay down and slept. Macsen had a dream. He was traveling northward over snowy mountains and wide plains. At last he came to a strange city, and from its windy harbor he took a ship to a green and pleasant island. He found himself wandering through this land, until he came to a region of crags, above the western sea. There he followed a river down to its mouth and found himself in front of a splendid palace, which looked out over green, white-capped waves.

Everything in this dream seemed more clear and more real than everyday life. The heavy doors swung open before him as he approached, so he entered. The great hall shone with silver and glittered with gems. There were youths playing board games, and a white-haired chieftain sat on an ivory throne.

But Macsen had eyes for none of these. One vision alone drew him forward. A young woman sat on a golden chair. She wore a shift of white silk, beneath a dress and cloak of gold brocade. Her pale face was framed by red

CONNECTIONS

• The figure of Macsen is probably based on the Spanish-born Magnus Maximus, commander of the Roman army in Britain. In A.D. 383, he led his troops to Rome and declared himself emperor.

• Many Britons (the Celtic ancestors of the Welsh) served with the Romans. Magnus might have appointed Eudaf, a British chieftain, to hold Segontium. He may well have married Eudaf's daughter, Elen.

• Did Britons really fight their way across Europe? We now know that one legion of the Roman army was known as the Segontienses.

• In 1282, the English invaded Wales. Their king, Edward I, knew Macsen's legend was still powerful. He ordered the building of a new castle at Caernarfon; it was just as splendid as the one in the old tale.

Near Caernarfon, in the green mountainous region of North Wales, the ruins and outlines of the Roman fortress of Segontium can still be seen today.

Macsen's search ended when he came upon the city of his dream, Segontium, in Arfon, where he found Elen.

curls. She looked up.

Suddenly the dream was interrupted by the baying and yelping of hounds. Macsen awoke with a start. The hunt was eager to be off, but the emperor turned home and would hunt no more.

"What troubles you, my lord?" asked his counselors when he returned. Macsen told them of his dream.

"Find this princess," he ordered. "Search the whole empire—search to the ends of the Earth."

On the dream quest

Messengers were sent out at once. For a whole year, they rode north, south, east, and west. They found nothing. In desperation, the emperor returned to the spot where he had rested from the hunt. Details of his dream journey came rushing back to him. He summoned his messengers and told them.

The messengers rode away to the north. They found the very mountains of his dream, the city, the harbor, the island... At last, they, too, came to the palace, and it was just as the emperor had described. It really did exist.

"Where are we?" they inquired of the guards. "This is Segontium in Arfon," the guards replied, "beneath the peaks of Eryri in the island of Britain."

The messengers entered the great hall, and all was just as the emperor had described. They fell on their knees before the girl and hailed her: "Empress of Rome!"

"You are mistaken," she replied. "My name is Elen, daughter of Eudaf."

"My lady, we are envoys of the Roman emperor," they explained hurriedly. "You have appeared in his dreams and he has fallen in love!"

"Indeed?" she laughed mockingly. "Then let the great man come and find me himself." The messengers returned to Rome and reported back to Macsen. The emperor gathered his best troops and rode north. At last Macsen saw the palace for himself. Elen smiled and welcomed him in, and his travel weariness disappeared. They fell in love and were soon married. Before long, Elen won the hearts of the emperor's troops. Macsen had new fortresses built in the island of Britain, with long, straight roads between them. For seven long years, the emperor stayed in Segontium.

Ruler once more

While the emperor was in Britain, Rome had no leader. Rivals took advantage, and one of them seized power. Macsen and Elen traveled south with their army. Rome was under siege, but Macsen could not capture it. At last, a band of British warriors rode in. Elen recognized the banners of her brothers, Cynan and Gadeon, who scaled the walls of Rome and killed its upstart ruler. Macsen ruled again, and the story of how he found Elen, his wife, was known wherever the legions marched.

Thor's Journey to Utgard

The Vikings lived in Scandinavia from A.D. 750 to 1100. In the early days, they believed in old Germanic gods and goddesses, such as Odin, father of the gods, and Thor, the god of war. Thor traveled from Asgard, the home of the gods, to the land of giants. Like Thor, the Vikings were warriors, who raided Europe in their longships and traveled to North America and the Middle East.

Two set out from Asgard, home of the gods. The first was the red-bearded Thor. He wore a glove of iron and wielded the deadly hammer called Mjöllnir, which crackled with blue lightning. Thor's companion, Loki, the trickster, lacked his strength, but made up for it in mischief and cunning. Where were they bound? To Utgard, the faraway fortress of the giants. The gods harnessed two goats to their wagon. The rumble of its wheels made thunder roll across the plain.

While they traveled through Midgard, the land of men, Thor and Loki came to a farmhouse and asked for shelter. They were welcomed by the poor farmer, Egil. He had scarcely enough food to feed his family, let alone hungry Thor. So Thor killed his own goats and cooked them. "Eat your fill," he said, "but don't chew the bones."

However, Egil's son Thjalfi was so very hungry that he chewed a bone. The next morning, Thor used magic to bring the bones back to life. When Thor saw that one of the goats was now lame because Thjalfi had chewed a bone, he flew into a rage and blamed him. He insisted that the young lad and his sister Roskva came with them.

Into the land of giants

They left Egil and walked until they reached the borders of Midgard. Ahead lay the gray sea and icy mountains. Finding an old boat, they rowed to the other shore and journeyed through a dark forest. At last, they became weary. Thjalfi spotted a house with five rooms. They slept there, but a raging storm shook the Earth. Their "house" was really a giant's glove, and the storm was his snoring! They saw him at first light—he was as big as a mountain.

"My name is Skrymir," he boomed.

The two gods and the two humans rowed toward the gloomy shores of the land of giants.

CONNECTIONS

• The old Germanic gods are commemorated in our names for the days of the week. "Thursday" is really Thor's day, and the German word for Thursday is Donnerstag, which means "thunder day."

• According to the Vikings, the Universe was held up by a huge ash tree called Yggdrasil.

• The Vikings believed there were several different worlds. The gods lived in Asgard, in a great hall called Valholl. Across a rainbow bridge lay Midgard, home of the humans. Utgard was the home of a race of giants, the gods' worst enemies. Beneath these upper worlds was Niflheim, an underworld of ice and mist.

The ruins of this Viking settlement in Scandinavia show the layout of a typical Viking house, where stories such as Thor's battles with giants would have been told in front of the open fire in the evening.

A stirring contest

They traveled with Skrymir for a day, but could not keep up with his mighty strides. At last, Thor lost his patience and slammed his hammer into the giant's skull as he slept. The giant merely murmured, "Oh, was that a falling leaf?"

Skrymir said farewell, and Thor and his companions set out to reach Utgard and the giant king Utgardaloki. "Prove you are worthy to eat at my table," the giant king jeered. The travelers agreed to take part in contests of skill. Thjalfi ran against their fastest runner, but lost. Loki lost an "eat-as-much-as-you-can" competition. Even Thor, for all his mighty strength, failed too. He could not empty the giant's drinking horn. He could not lift up the giant's cat, or even wrestle his old grandmother to the ground. Thor was ashamed, but he need not have been.

Thjalfi peered into the doorway of the strange house with its five chambers. Thor stood guard with his hammer, Mjöllnir.

The king explained that Thjalfi's opponent was Thought, with whom no one can catch up. Loki's opponent was really Fire, which consumes everything. As for Thor, the drinking horn had been constantly refilled by the sea.

The cat? It was really the Midgard Serpent, whose coils surround the Earth. And the grandmother? She was Old Age, and none of us can beat her. "Oh, and by the way," added the king, "Skrymir was really me. I fended off your hammer blows by shielding myself with a mountain."

Thor reached for his hammer again—but the fortress and giants vanished. The two gods and two humans stood alone on a windswept plain. "Let's head for home," said Loki. "There will always be a new day for fighting giants."

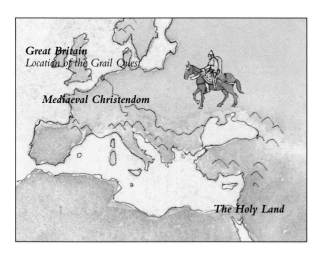

Great Britain
Location of the Grail Quest

Mediaeval Christendom

The Holy Land

Quest for the Holy Grail

The search for the Holy Grail is one of the best-known "Arthurian" legends. These tales are about a man called Arthur, who may have been a war leader of the British Celts from A.D. 516 to 537.

Merlin was a wizard. Just by staring into the glowing embers of a fire or watching the clouds racing by, he could see the pattern of future events unfolding. Long ago, Merlin had foretold that the boy, Arthur, would become the High King, and bring peace and justice to the island of Britain. He had also warned of darker signs—of betrayal, sorcery, and battles. All of these prophecies came true in their time.

One of Merlin's most powerful visions had been that of knights journeying across the land, searching for the Holy Grail. This was a precious cup, Merlin explained to Arthur, which had been brought to Britain long ago. It contained drops of Jesus Christ's blood, which had been caught as he was dying on the cross. Only the purest knight would ever be able to find the Holy Grail.

The quest begins

Each year at Whitsun, the Christian festival of the Holy Spirit, Arthur summoned his knights to sit at the Round Table, at his castle in Camelot. One year, after a splendid tournament, the knights entered the great hall, talking of horses, helmets, and lances.

There was a roar of thunder and a dazzling, radiant light. The knights felt themselves filled with the spirit of God. There appeared a cup, draped in shimmering, white silk. This was indeed the Holy Grail. The vision hovered and then vanished from sight. King Arthur was awestruck, but saddened, too. He knew this was the start of the quest prophesied years ago by Merlin. His knights would be scattered far and wide, and many brave men would never return to Camelot.

Testing journeys

Sir Gawain the Courteous, nephew of the king, leaped to his feet. "I wish to seek this Grail, and may God grant me fulfillment of this quest."

He buckled on his armor and lifted his great shield. His horse's hooves echoed around the great stone walls of the court as he rode away.

Many other knights followed Gawain. In the years that followed, they traveled through dark, tangled forests of oak and bramble. They crossed rushing rivers and became lost in misty marshes. They battled with evil knights and phantoms. They rescued people who were in danger and people who were placed under enchantments. Each deed they carried out was a test, not of their courage, but of the purity of their souls. All desired to see the Grail, since only this would cure all their ills and bring true peace of mind.

The journeying lasted many years, and the knights who survived grew grizzled and worn. Even bold Gawain failed in the quest. Exhausted knights straggled back to Camelot and told King Arthur of their adventures.

Lancelot's quest

Most people believed Sir Lancelot would be the knight who succeeded, as he was the bravest knight ever to sit at the Round Table. But his heart was not pure. He carried a grievance, like a nagging wound. Lancelot was the greatest friend of King Arthur, yet he had fallen in love with Queen Guinevere. This love had brought misery and discord to Camelot, and weakened

The Holy Grail was sought all over the British Isles by King Arthur's trusted knights.

As Sir Galahad knelt before the Holy Grail at the castle of Carbonek, there arose a vision of Jesus Christ.

struck by lightning. He was unconscious for many weeks, and when he awoke from his deep sleep, he felt that he had been healed.

Lancelot's son Sir Galahad continued the search for the Holy Grail, meeting with other knights on his travels. Sir Bors and Sir Percival were greatly honored, for Galahad completed the last stage of the quest with them.

Galahad and glory

All the knights were brave, but young Galahad alone had never been selfish or vengeful. His soul was pure. He and his companions came to a land ruled by a king called Pelles, and there they discovered a magical castle called Carbonek.

At Carbonek, Galahad achieved the quest. He was shown the Holy Grail, which had been set by four angels upon a table of solid silver. Out of the cup came a vision of Christ, with bleeding wounds. A feeling of joy spread across the land. Galahad, Bors, and Percival were told to take the Grail by ship to the faraway city of Sarras, where people did not worship Christ. Galahad prayed for them, and he became filled with holiness. When he died, his soul and the Grail were carried to heaven in a dazzling blaze of light.

the rule of the king. On one of his journeys, Lancelot met a fair knight on a distant shore. Listening to the stranger's story, he realized that it was his own long-lost son, Sir Galahad. They rode together for half a year before parting. Lancelot was then granted a vision of the Grail, but when he tried to grasp it, he fell backward, as if

The quest for the Holy Grail was the greatest triumph of King Arthur's court and his knights. The old days of magic and mystery were passing. Merlin had known that he would be the last of the great wizards.

CONNECTIONS

• If Arthur existed, he may have been a leader who fought Saxon invaders. Over 700 years later, he was known as a great Christian king.

• The idea of the Grail probably dates back to pre-Christian times, when many Celtic myths tell of a magic cauldron that brings healing and life.

• The character of Lancelot is a French addition to the Arthurian legends. He represents the ideal medieval knight. Knights tried to follow a code of noble behavior, which is known as chivalry.

• Many different versions of the Grail legend were told in the late Middle Ages. In some of them, it is Percival, not Galahad, who fulfills the quest.

• The old tales do not say where the city of Sarras is. Most people assume it is in the Near East; it could be Jerusalem.

The Chalice Well at Glastonbury is named after the cup, or chalice, used by Christians during the Eucharist service. Like the Holy Grail, the chalice is linked with the story of Jesus Christ.

The Journey of Doom

The Song of the Nibelungs, from which this story comes, was written down in Germany about 800 years ago. The unknown author tells an exciting story about the Christian kings, queens, and knights of his own day. But he based his tale on much older myths and legends from Scandinavia and Germany, and this is why we also read of dragon's blood, magic, and water spirits.

Kriemhild was princess of Burgundy, a pleasant land to the west of the river Rhine. Her eldest brother, Gunther, was king of Burgundy. Far to the north, where the Rhine meets the sea, lived a bold young prince of the Lowlands named Siegfried. Hearing of Kriemhild's great beauty, Siegfried decided to seek her hand in marriage. Dressed in golden armor, he rode to Burgundy.

Siegfried made a princely impression as he galloped into the fine old city of Worms.

"Who is he?" whispered one noble lady admiringly.

"A famous hero," replied another. "He killed the King of the Nibelungs and carried off his fabulous treasure."

"They say he also took a magic cloak, that makes the wearer invisible! And I heard that he bathed in dragon's blood and cannot be harmed!"

Kriemhild fell in love with Siegfried at once, and he with her. Once the two were married, he gave her his marvelous hoard of treasure. Time and again, Siegfried proved his friendship to the Burgundian royal family. However, his loyalty was rewarded only with jealousy.

The beautiful princess, Kriemhild, rode east along the Danube valley.

As Siegfried grew more powerful, Gunther and her other brothers began to complain about Siegfried's growing power in the land. One of their knights, a grim-faced warrior called Hagen, who was also their uncle, decided to do away with Siegfried. He tricked Kriemhild into revealing the spot on Siegfried's body that remained unprotected. Siegfried was murdered while he was out hunting, and Hagen and Kriemhild's brothers took the treasure and sank it in the river Rhine. Kriemhild's grief was terrifying. Her eyes stared wildly at her brothers. If her own kinsmen betrayed her like this, who would come to

CONNECTIONS

• In older Scandinavian tales, Siegfried, the hero, is said to be the son of Odin, the greatest of the gods, rather than a prince.

• In Germanic mythology, the Nibelungs were a race of dwarfs. In this version of the tale, theirs is a human kingdom. However, the term is also used to describe anyone who holds their treasure, be it Siegfried or the royal family of Burgundy.

• The Burgundians were a Germanic people who traveled westward across the river Rhine in the A.D. 400s. Their lands encompassed Worms, Geneva, and Lyon.

• Etzel is the German name of Attila the Hun, the greatest warlord of the Huns, an Asian people whose warriors attacked Europe in the A.D. 400s. They conquered land from the river Danube to China's borders.

The Cathedral of Worms, one of the cities occupied by the Burgundian peoples from around the A.D. 400s. Their lands were later merged with those of the Franks, a West Germanic people.

her aid? After a year, her pain seemed sharper than ever, and she dreamed of revenge. One day, messengers arrived from Etzel, King of the Huns, asking Kriemhild if she would marry him. To the surprise of many, she agreed. So Kriemhild rode east along the Danube valley, with a bodyguard of the finest knights. There she married Etzel in a splendid ceremony. However, the lovely Kriemhild planned wickedness and invited her brothers to visit her. Hagen was suspicious—however, he and a thousand Burgundian knights rode out of the city of Worms.

Soon they reached the river Danube. There, Hagen met with beautiful maidens called nixies—water spirits who tell the future. Suddenly they reared up like ghouls and warned that all who went to Etzel's court would die, but Hagen and the Burgundian knights rode onward.

The Burgundians needed to cross the Danube, but the river was in full flood. As a Bavarian guard came to ferry them over, Hagen quarreled with him. He struck off his head and threw it into the rushing waters.

"A fine journey this will be," muttered the knights.

No turning back

The Bavarians, outraged by the murder at the crossing, launched a bloody attack on the Burgundian travelers. There was terrible slaughter. And still, Hagen and his men rode onward. Reaching Pöchlar, they set up camp by the castle of the lord, Rüdiger, who owed allegiance to Etzel.

Rüdiger joined the knights and they rode through the dark forests of Austria to the land of the Huns. On Midsummer's Eve, Hagen and the Burgundian knights reached Etzel's palace. The newcomers were greeted

graciously. But, like a spider in her web, Kriemhild plotted to trap her guests. She bribed Etzel's knights to take her side. Soon, a fierce and terrible battle broke out. Huns fought Burgundians, swarming over the courtyards and ramparts, and hundreds lay dead.

Terrible end

Pressed in by the Huns, the Burgundians blockaded themselves in the great hall. Then Kriemhild, laughing insanely, ordered the hall to be set ablaze. The few who escaped kept fighting. Rüdiger owed allegiance to Etzel and was killed fighting his new friends, the Burgundians.

Kriemhild seized a sword and struck off Hagen's head. Silence fell as everyone was frozen in horror. Hildebrand stepped forward, a veteran in Etzel's service and friend of Hagen. Kriemhild held out a hand to him, expecting support. But he raised his great sword and swung it at the queen. She, too, fell to the floor, and her dying vision was of smoke darkening the sky, blotting out all memories of her dear Siegfried.

Hagen encountered the nixies, who could see into the future. They brought him a grim message of death.

The Wandering Odysseus

The ancient Greeks believed that the gods and goddesses lived on Mount Olympus, high in the clouds. They were always interfering in the lives of human beings—as Odysseus discovered. Odysseus was cunning, brave, and quick with his sword. His name means "angry," and it is said that he fought in the Trojan wars in around 1220 B.C. The tale was written by Homer in 750 B.C.

The kingdom of Ithaca had no king. Once it had been ruled by the great Odysseus, the best of kings and the bravest of all the Greeks. But he had sailed away long ago, to fight the Trojans in a terrible war. Was the king dead or alive? Nobody knew. Penelope, his wife, longed for news, and so did their son Telemachus.

CONNECTIONS

• Odysseus' story passed from Greece to Italy, and he was known to the ancient Romans as "Ulysses."
• Some of the places in the tale really existed. Ithaca is an island off Western Greece, now called Itháki. The remains of the city of Troy were discovered in Northwest Turkey. Cythera is a southern Greek island, today known as Kíthira.
• At the time when Homer was writing down the story of Odysseus, many Greeks were sailing around the coasts of the Black Sea and the Mediterranean. That is why people loved to hear tales about seafaring and adventure.
• The story of Odysseus is so famous that any long period of wandering or travel is now called an "Odyssey."

The ruins of the city gates at the eastern edge of Troy, a prosperous city that existed from 1800–1200 B.C., in Northwest Turkey. The conquest of Troy marked the start of Odysseus' wanderings.

"Is there still no sign of their sails?" the queen would ask the watchman each day. The years passed, but the king's ships never appeared on the horizon. The palace became full of intrigue. Courtiers ate and drank greedily, plotting to win the empty throne for themselves.

Zeus was the father of the gods and ruler of the skies. Armed with thunder and lightning, he would hurl down thunderbolts from Mount Olympus when he was angry. He knew only too well that Odysseus was still alive. The king's delay was due to all the other gods and goddesses, who were always squabbling among themselves. No sooner had one of them set Odysseus on his homeward course, than another one sent him astray.

Dangerous dreams

After the Greeks' victory at Troy, Odysseus had sailed south with his fleet and raided the city of Ismarus, losing six of his men in a battle. He then set course for home, but near the island of Cythera, his ships were blown off course. They came to the sleepy land where the lotus plant grew. When his crew ate its honeyed fruit, it brought them sweet dreams and they lingered there lazily and forgot all about the journey home.

"Come to your senses, fools!" shouted Odysseus. Grabbing rope from the ships, he bound their wrists and dragged them back on board.

The Cyclopes

Odysseus and his crew needed meat and fresh water, and sheep and goats were available at their next port of call. The trouble was, this land was ruled by monstrous one-eyed giants called the Cyclopes. One of them, Polyphemus, trapped some of the voyagers in his cave and he began to dash out their brains and eat them. Odysseus made the monster drunk with wine, until he staggered

When Odysseus and his hungry men raided Hyperion's island to steal cattle for food, Zeus sent a thunderbolt to sink Odysseus' ship.

Ithaca to see the glimmering fires of their homes. But Odysseus' crew had become curious. What priceless treasure did the bag contain? Nuggets of gold and silver rings? While Odysseus slept, they opened the bag. Gales and hurricanes poured out and drove them all back to Aeolia, across the foam-streaked waves. Aeolus was enraged. "You must be detested by the gods," he roared. "Leave here now and never return!" Weary and downcast, the Greeks dug their oars deep into sluggish water, for Aeolus had stilled the winds. After six days, they came to an island of cannibals, who attacked them with rocks and speared the sailors as if they were fish, then ate them for supper. It seemed to the sailors that Aeolus must have spoken the truth.

around helplessly. He blinded the beast, driving a red-hot stake into the sizzling eye socket, and so the voyagers made their escape. As they sailed away, Polyphemus threw huge rocks into the sea. Now, Polyphemus was the son of the god Poseidon, shaker of the Earth and lord of the sea. For this act, Poseidon vowed to seek revenge on Odysseus and his men.

On a floating island called Aeolia, Odysseus met Aeolus, King of the Winds. The voyager was given a present: a leather bag that imprisoned all but the fairest winds. The Greeks bade farewell to Aeolus. After ten nights, powerful breezes had carried them close enough to the coast of

To Hades and back

Only one ship escaped from the cannibals, that of brave Odysseus. He came at last to safe harbor in the island of Aeaea, where he and his crew rested.

Exploring the island, one group found a stone house that was surrounded by lions and wolves. This was the home of the witch Circe. She lured the sailors in with her beautiful singing, and changed the poor fellows into pigs. Hermes, messenger of the gods, was sent to the rescue just in time. He gave Odysseus a magic ▶

The Wandering Odysseus

herb that prevented him from being bewitched. Circe was impressed and was soon charmed by Odysseus, who persuaded her to turn the pigs back into men.

He begged her to use her magic to send him home. She agreed on one condition: that he first visited the chilly shores of Hades, the underworld. The crew were dismayed, but set off once more. Fog drifted in, and on the edge of everlasting night, Odysseus called up the ghostly souls of the dead. He was told about the troubles in Ithaca. Odysseus now sailed back to Circe.

"Odysseus, I promised to get you home and so I shall," Circe sighed, "but many more dangers still await you."

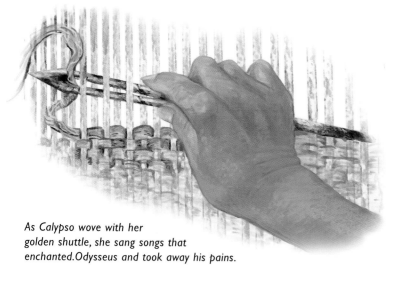

As Calypso wove with her golden shuttle, she sang songs that enchanted.Odysseus and took away his pains.

Sure enough, Odysseus and his men were soon facing them. First, they had to sail past the Sirens, who lure seafarers to their death with their beautiful, haunting melodies. Cunning Odysseus plugged his crew's ears with wax, and then lashed himself to the mast, so that he could hear their singing without leaping from the ship.

Later in the voyage, Odysseus and his men raided a herd of island cattle belonging to Hyperion. Now, as hungry as the sailors were, they should never have crossed Hyperion, for he was the Sun god. He cried out for vengeance, and mighty Zeus had little choice but to obey. A thunderbolt hit the brave ship, and it finally sank beneath the waves.

Calypso's island

Only one man survived, and that was Odysseus himself. Along with the timbers of his wrecked ship, he was washed up on the sands of another island. As he revived, he saw seabirds wheeling in the sky, above the mouth of a cave—the home of the beautiful nymph Calypso. Here

there were crystal springs and the sweet-scented smoke of a cedarwood and juniper fire. Calypso sang her sweet songs as she wove with a golden shuttle.

Odysseus felt his aches and pains die away under her enchantment. Every day he dreamed of returning home, but he was powerless to leave, because the gods were arguing about his fate, as usual.

"Odysseus must be allowed to return to Ithaca before there is serious trouble there," insisted Athene, the daughter of Zeus and goddess of wisdom.

"Oh, very well," rumbled Zeus wearily. He sent the messenger god, Hermes, swooping down over the waves. Hermes broke Calypso's spell at once and allowed Odysseus to sail away on a small raft.

Homeward bound

After eighteen days of steering by the stars, Odysseus sighted the land of the Phaeacians, its coastline wreathed in mist. At that very moment, he was seen by Poseidon.

"Doom and damnation!" bellowed the god. "Why has this wretch been allowed to escape yet again? Now is my chance for revenge!" Poseidon whipped up towering waves, which bore down on the raft. Wrecked on jagged rocks, Odysseus managed to swim into the mouth of a river. Raw and bleeding, he fell asleep on the shore. The Phaeacian king's lovely daughter found him there. She and her father welcomed him to their palace, which gleamed with bronze, silver, and gold.

"Who is this stranger?" went the whisper. "Is he a god in disguise?" Odysseus was persuaded to reveal who he was and tell of his wanderings. When he had finished his story, there was an awed silence in the Phaeacian palace. Eventually, the king spoke, and his voice was filled with a new respect for his guest. He promised to provide Odysseus with a fine ship for the journey home. As the morning star gave way to the rose-pink light of dawn, the wanderer's ship at last reached Ithaca, his homeland.

There were many more adventures and brave deeds, but in the end, Odysseus, with the help of his son, Telemachus, brought back order to his kingdom and happiness to his wife, Penelope. He had been away from home for ten years, but his wife had waited faithfully for him all that time. His wanderings were over at last.

Odysseus had only a small raft to carry him over rough seas when he faced the final stage of his journey home. He was determined to reach Ithaca, despite the obstacles Poseidon, the sea god, threw in his path.

From Troy to Rome

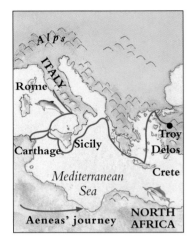

This story is called the Aeneid. *It was written by the Roman poet, Virgil (70–19 B.C.), who died just before the work was finished, after traveling from Athens to Rome by sea. It tells a legend like that of Odysseus, only the hero of this story is a Trojan, not a Greek. He and his followers wandered for many years before they arrived in Italy and founded the state that eventually grew into the Roman Empire.*

This tale begins with the great city of Troy lying in ruins, its people put to the sword by the Greeks. Some of the Trojans fled to Italy, where they founded a new city after fighting. The greatest Trojan hero of them all was Aeneas, son of Anchises and Venus, goddess of love.

A black pall of smoke filled the sky as Aeneas carried his elderly father from Troy. Hearts heavy with grief, the surviving Trojan people went down to their ships. Few dared to look back as they set sail across the Aegean. On the island of Delos, they nursed their wounds. One morning, they went to

Dido watches as the ships set sail from Carthage.

worship at the temple of Apollo, when a mighty earthquake shook the island. They heard a great roar, followed by these words: "Brave Trojans, do not despair. Set sail from here. One day you will found a mighty city and your descendants will rule a great empire."

CONNECTIONS
• The Romans shared many myths, legends, and gods with the Greeks. Jupiter, for example, was the Greek god, Zeus.
• By Virgil's lifetime, Greece had come under Roman rule. The poet wanted to create a Roman epic like *The Odyssey* of the Greeks. His aim was to honor Rome, and to suggest that its emperors were descended from the Trojan heroes.
• Troy was a city in what is now Western Turkey. It was probably conquered by the Greeks in the 1200s B.C.

Carthage was founded by the Phoenecians, destroyed in 146 B.C., and was rebuilt by the Romans ten years before Virgil's death.

The search for a home
But where should they go? Anchises pulled at his white beard. "Ancient legends say that we Trojans originally came from the island of Crete. We should sail southward."

So they sailed across the Sea of Crete and landed on the island. They felled trees and began to build a new stone citadel. But the land was sick with plague and drought. Surely Crete could not provide a lasting home?

One night during a full moon, Aeneas dreamed of the gods and heard their voices telling him where the destiny of his people lay. Relief flooded through him.

"To Italy!" shouted Aeneas, as dawn paled the sky. Soon, their ships sailed westward to the Ionian Sea.

When they raided cattle on one island, the Trojans were attacked by foul bird-women, the Harpies of hell.

"Keep away from our lands," they shrieked. "The gods have told us you are bound for Italy. Go there!"

The Trojans came upon another land, where Cyclopes bellowed from the shore. The voyagers only just escaped a terrible fate—these one-eyed giants loved eating human bodies and crunched bones in their massive jaws. On the island of Sicily, old Anchises died and Aeneas wept, remembering the golden days of Troy. There seemed to be no safe havens any more. While they sailed around the island, the Trojan ships ran into a tempest, brewed up by Juno, the queen of heaven. She had always detested the Trojans. Only seven ships survived, and these were driven onto the white sands of North Africa.

Queen Dido in love

Here, where they landed, the Phoenician queen Dido was building the city of Carthage. Powerful and wise, she welcomed the Trojans with a lavish banquet, with wine and music. Dido listened as Aeneas told of their journey.

"You must indeed be favored by the gods, to have survived so many disasters!" she sighed, staring at him.

At that very moment, the goddess Venus made Dido fall desperately in love with Aeneas, her son. "Stay here with us, Trojan," pleaded Dido. "Share my city and my throne."

Aeneas was falling in love with Dido. But while he lingered in Africa, Jupiter, king of the gods, grew angry. He issued an order: Aeneas was to sail to Italy at once. Reluctantly, the Trojan agreed, struggling against his heart.

As the fleet raised anchor, Dido was consumed with fury and grief. She made offerings to her gods, but the holy water turned black and the wine changed to blood. No hope was left. She killed herself and her body was burnt in public on a high funeral pyre.

In the land of Hades, Aeneas met many of his dead loved ones.

To the land of the dead

When Aeneas finally reached Italy, he consulted a prophetess, who revealed a route into Hades, the shadowy home of dead souls. In this land of gloomy forests and howling monsters, Aeneas saw the spirit of the pitiful Dido and wept when he discovered her fate. He saw the ghost of his father, Anchises, who told him the Romans would conquer Carthage, Greece, and the world. Aeneas would be the ancestor of Julius Caesar, the brave general.

So Aeneas made one final journey to Latina, the fairest region of Italy, which was later the heart of ancient Rome, to fight the Latina king. At last, Aeneas won and married the king's daughter.

The King Who Could Not Conquer Death

Stories about Gilgamesh were first told by the Sumerians, who lived in what is now Iraq. Gilgamesh was a mythical hero, based on an Uruk king who lived 4,000 years ago. This tale comes from the Epic of Gilgamesh, *which was first written on clay tablets.*

Gilgamesh the king was a fine figure: part man, part god. He was as strong as a bull in its prime and as willful as the wind. Gilgamesh was ruler of Uruk, and in that fine city he built strong walls and a splendid temple. But now his heart was broken, for Enkidu was dead—Enkidu, the wild man. He had been made from clay by the goddess Aruru, to challenge the growing power of King Gilgamesh. Enkidu had wrestled with him in hand-to-hand combat. But the two soon made peace and became the best of friends.

Plains and mountains

When Enkidu died of a fever, Gilgamesh wept bitterly, and left his beloved and beautiful city in deep despair. Where now were his royal robes and his courtiers? Gilgamesh wandered across the plains and grasslands, dressed in rough skins, hunting wild animals. One night, woken from his dreams, he saw that fierce lions were circling him. Before they could set upon him, he attacked them with sword and ax. He could kill savage lions, but he could not cure the aching in his heart.

If Enkidu could die, then so could he. Why must all things come to an end? Why must all life fade away? Gilgamesh could only think of one person who might know the answer, and his name was Utnapishtim the Faraway. Utnapishtim, it was said, had cheated death. He had gone to the paradise of Dilmun, beyond the garden of the sun, where the gods had granted him the gift of eternal life.

Gilgamesh set out to find him. At last he came to the mountains of Mashu, beyond which is the domain of the rising sun. The mountains were guarded by the terrifying Scorpions, who were half men, half dragons.

"Why do you travel across land and sea?" questioned the Scorpions.

"I grieve for Enkidu, and I need to know why people must die," answered Gilgamesh sadly. "I seek Utnapishtim the Faraway."

"Then enter the gate of the mountain."

For a long while, the awful darkness under the mountain hemmed him in. He was stifled, he could see nothing. And then, at last, he felt a breeze and saw the glorious sun.

The garden of the sun

On the other side of the mountain, the plants in the garden of the sun were festooned with sparkling gems, with blue lapis lazuli and creamy pearls. Shamash the sun god blazed there. "Gilgamesh," he said, "you will never find a way to conquer death."

Siduri, the wine maiden who sat beside the sea, said the same: "No one may live forever."

"Then where may I find Utnapishtim?" pleaded Gilgamesh. "For I believe that only he can tell me the secrets of life and death."

"He lives beyond the ocean. The sun can cross the ocean, but the likes of you cannot cross the waters of death and live."

"I have to go, for I am in despair," insisted Gilgamesh.

Gilgamesh braved the fierce Scorpions, the terrifying guardians of the mountains of Mashu, in his quest for immortality.

The flowers in the garden of the sun sparkled with precious, life-giving gems.

"Enkidu is dead and I fear to follow him."

Siduri admitted that there was a ferryman.

"His name is Urshanabi, and he alone can take you over the water." So Gilgamesh found Urshanabi, who ferried him over to the paradise of Dilmun. In this way, the king survived the waters of death.

The wisdom of Utnapishtim

On that distant, eastern shore, Gilgamesh was challenged by the wise Utnapishtim.

"Who are you—stranger, friend, or foe? Why do you wear rough animal skins? Why are you so thin and pale?"

"I am Gilgamesh, King of Uruk," he replied. "I am stricken with grief for my dear friend Enkidu. I have traveled over freezing mountains and burning plains. I am starving and my bones are aching. I have come to ask you a question. Tell me, why must people die?"

Utnapishtim sighed. "Nothing lasts forever in this world. Buildings eventually crumble and fall. Worldly goods perish. Dragonflies may take on a new lease of life and grow shimmering wings, but like us they will turn to dust."

"Not you," insisted Gilgamesh. "You have been given the gift of eternal life. Why?"

Utnapishtim told him this story: "Long ago, I lived in Shurrupak, beside the river Euphrates. It was a busy city, and the tiresome babble of its citizens infuriated the god Enli. He vowed to drown the world and everything in it. But first, the god Ea secretly warned me to build ▶

Gilgamesh dived deep into the sea, searching for a magical plant like a thorny rose that grew on the seabed. It was said to make the old become young again and make the weary become strong.

The beautiful city of Uruk, which the great king Gilgamesh built and ruled for his people.

a great boat. I did this and loaded it with my family, with provisions, with all the animals in the world. Then the god sent a great flood and a mighty storm, and the land was lost beneath the waves.

"For six days, a great rainstorm raged. I searched for land but found none, until the boat struck the slopes of Mount Nisir. I released a dove, but she found no dry land where she could settle, and returned.

"I released a swallow, and she, too, came home to roost. I released a raven, and she, at last, found dry land, for the waters were receding.

"Soon we were walking on dry land. I made offerings to the gods, and they rewarded me with everlasting life. Gilgamesh, just as flood waters drain from the land, so people have their day and disappear from this world."

The return to Uruk

Gilgamesh felt a great weariness descend upon him, and he fell asleep for seven days. Utnapishtim awoke him, since he was in danger of dying in this long sleep. Gilgamesh, king of Uruk, was then washed in a clear spring, and his travel-stained skins were exchanged for fresh clothes. Before he left, Gilgamesh was told of a magical plant that grows on the seabed, thorny like a rose. It was said to make the weary strong and the old young again. So he dived down for it, and vowed to bring it back to Uruk. Gilgamesh set off for home with Urshanabi, the ferryman. They returned through the gate of the mountains and headed out across the plain, but the journeying was now much faster. On the way, a water serpent stole the magical plant from Gilgamesh while he bathed in a pool.

"I have achieved nothing," groaned Gilgamesh.

"Look, Gilgamesh," replied the ferryman, "ahead lies the wonderful city of Uruk. This was your great achievement, and this is how you will be remembered. You cannot live forever like the gods, for part of you is mortal man. Yet, your deeds on Earth will bring you a kind of immortality, for you will live in the memory of future generations."

Remembered through eternity

Gilgamesh asked stonemasons to carve the story of his journey in stone, so that people in future generations could learn what he had done and give thanks to the gods. When he died, the people of Uruk lamented and grieved, just as he had done for Enkidu. But the spirit and the memory of Gilgamesh lived on in their hearts, although his body was turning to dust in the great stone tomb.

CONNECTIONS

• The story told here is taken from the second half of the *Epic of Gilgamesh*. The first half tells how Enkidu, the wild man, was created and how he came to Uruk. It tells how Enkidu and Gilgamesh cut down a sacred cedar tree guarded by an evil monster named Humbaba, and how they killed the storm-driven Bull of Heaven.

• Uruk was a real city. In the Bible it is called Erech. It lay near the modern city of Warka. Shurrupak is known today as Fara.

• Utnapishtim predates Noah, the Biblical character who builds an ark. Flood myths are common in all parts of the world, suggesting that rising sea levels caused major floods in ancient times, perhaps as a result of climate change.

The rivers Tigris and Euphrates start in Turkey and run southward through Syria and Iraq to the sea. It was in their fertile valleys that people first learned to farm, and it was here that the world's first cities and empires were founded.

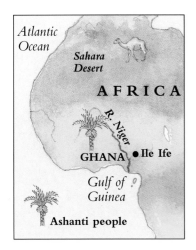

Travels of a Trickster

In myths and legends around the world, heroes are praised for their cunning as much as their bravery. One such hero is Kwaku Ananse, a spider-man who loves to play tricks. This story about him was one of many that were passed down from one generation to the next by storytellers in the ancient kingdom of Ashanti. These are still to be heard in the villages of Ghana, in West Africa.

Telling a tale is a little like spinning a spider's web. If its silken threads are strong, all who listen become ensnared. Long ago, there were no storytellers and no tales for the telling. Nyame, the sky god, kept all the world's stories locked in a wooden box, high above the clouds. Kwaku Ananse, who was both spider and man, wanted them very badly.

"I could tell those stories to people," he complained to his wife, Aso. She looked up from her cooking pot.

"Oh, you're all talk, you know. Why don't you do something about it?"

The spider's quest

Ananse traveled to see the sky god and asked if he could buy the stories. The sky god snorted in derision, causing a raging storm to blow through the Great Forest far below.

"Sell my stories? To a poor fool like you? You would not know what to do with them."

"Oh, yes I would," declared Ananse. "I am as clever as you are, and I can pay any price you ask."

"You will have to travel very far," said Nyame.

"Don't I have eight strong limbs?" retorted Ananse.

"Then travel through the Great Forest. Seek out its rarest creatures and bring them to me. Let's see... I shall require

Onini, the giant python, and Osebo, the sharp-fanged leopard... Mmotia, the fickle sprite, catch her—if you can! And what about Mmoboro, that hornet with the fearful sting? Prove yourself to me, and the stories shall be yours."

Ananse returned to Earth. When Aso heard of his tasks, she raised her eyebrows. "Well, it's lucky that I've got some brains, at least," she sighed. "We'll figure out what to do."

The python and the leopard

Ananse bade Aso farewell and traveled through the dark forest. He came at last to a wide, muddy river. He carried with him a long pole and some twine. As he strolled along the banks, he pretended to be having a conversation with someone. He made sure that Onini heard every word: "Onini, as long as this pole? Surely not!"

"I bet you he is!"

Under a tangle of vines, he found the snake, sleek and coiled. "I am the longest python in the world," boasted the giant-sized reptile.

"Prove it!" jeered Ananse.

The great snake uncoiled and lay beside Ananse's pole to be measured. In an instant, Ananse had tied Onini to the pole. He journeyed back from the forest and handed over the snake to the sky god.

CONNECTIONS
• Kwaku Ananse was first turned into a spider as a punishment for his trickery. Many African myths and traditional tales are about animals who have human characteristics, or about humans who have become animals.
• Another cunning animal hero of West African tales was a rabbit. He became known to African Americans as "Br'er Rabbit," and is a popular cartoon character.
• A calabash is a large gourd. Dried and hollowed, it is used as a container and water carrier in West Africa. Smaller gourds are used as drinking cups.
• Stories told by West African storytellers are still called *anansesem*, or "spider-tales."

This tale belongs to the Ashanti people who live in Ghana in West Africa. In the 1700s and 1800s, their kingdom grew powerful and wealthy from trading with gold.

On his next mission, Ananse had to travel even farther, tracking the leopard Osebo for days on end. He peered into the branches of trees, where leopards drag their prey. Near one trunk, he found fresh paw marks and dug a pit. That night, the leopard crashed into Ananse's trap.

"Let me out," snarled Osebo the next morning.

"You'll kill me if I do," laughed Ananse.

"Oh no, I won't!"

"Then, let me tie you with this rope and haul you out of the pit." Ananse tied one end of the rope to the leopard and the other to a bent palm sapling. He let this spring upward, yanking Osebo into the air. Ananse killed him and carried him to the sky god.

The wooden doll

Ananse's third journey was hot and sticky. At last, he found a huge old rubber tree, which was a dancing place for forest sprites. From his bundle, he pulled out a wooden doll and covered it with sticky sap from the tree. Then he pulled out a bowl of delicious mashed yams, put it in the doll's hands, and hid. When the sprite came by, she ate the yams, but stuck fast to the doll's body. How she complained when Ananse carried her off to the sky god!

Ananse's last journey took him to the edge of the Great Forest, where angry hornets swarmed around a bank of red earth. He filled a calabash with river water, and sprinkled it over them and himself. Then he pulled a leaf from a plantain tree and placed it over his head, as if he was sheltering from the rain. "Dear me," he said loudly. "The rains are very heavy this year! Hornets, take shelter in my calabash!"

In they buzzed and Ananse sealed the opening at once. Weary but triumphant, he returned to the sky god.

Nyame, the sky god, grumbled as he fetched the wooden box, making thunder crash around him. He called together all the chiefs and warriors down below, and stood them in a line before Ananse and his wife, Aso.

"Kwaku Ananse has triumphed in his quest!" he proclaimed from the clouds.

"Thanks to me!" muttered Aso under her breath.

"From now on, the spider-man shall be honored all over the Great Forest as the chief teller of tales."

He remains so to this very day, for people still say of a talented storyteller, "Oh, he's a real Kwaku Ananse."

Kwaku Ananse catapulted the snarling leopard from his cunning trap and killed him.

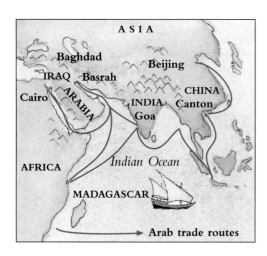

Arab trade routes

The Seven Voyages of Sindbad

Tales from the Thousand and One Nights *were a series of fairy stories and legends collected in Persia (now Iran) and translated into Arabic in A.D. 850. The version we know today was probably written down in Cairo, Egypt, in 1450.*

There was once a beautiful young woman, whose cleverness saved her from a dreadful fate. Her name was Shahrazad, and she was held captive by King Shahriya. Each evening, he threatened to have her executed at dawn the next day. Shahrazad spent each night telling tales to her sister. The king was fascinated to hear her voice. Shahrazad made sure that by the time the sun rose each day, she had not reached the end of her story. In order to hear what happened next in the tale, the king had to allow her to live for one more day.

For 1,001 nights, Shahrazad stayed alive by telling her tales. At last, the king repented of his wickedness. He ordered her life to be spared and the two became married. Some of Shahrazad's most exciting tales were about a sailor called Sindbad.

Sindbad clung to the leg of the giant roc as it carried him far away from the island.

Whales and a washtub

Sindbad was a merchant of Baghdad, who lived in the days when Haroun al-Raschid ruled that splendid city. Have you heard of his travels? His first voyage began when he traveled down-river to the port of Basrah and hired a captain and crew. The wooden ship was laden with bales of silk and sacks of coffee beans. Sindbad prospered in his trade and became rich.

One day Sindbad's captain came across a sandy island, which looked as if it was covered in green plants. They all went to shore on the island and lit a fire. Then, just as they were beginning to explore the island, the captain yelled, "Allah, have mercy upon us!"

The whole island was heaving up into the air. Really, this was not land at all, but the back of a great whale, festooned in seaweed. The whale was enraged by the fire. As it began to plunge back into the depths, the crew scrambled back on board the ship. Sindbad leapt into a wooden washtub and was soon swept away from his companions. In the end, that tub was washed up on an island shore. From there, Sindbad found his way to a port, where eventually he met up with his old shipmates. He took a handsome profit home to Baghdad.

The diamonds of the roc

Still dreaming of adventure and distant horizons, Sindbad set out again. Soon he was in trouble again. Left behind on an island, he came across a large white dome that looked like a building. However, this was no building, but a bird's egg, the biggest in the world. It belonged to the roc, an enormous bird so monstrously huge that its wings blocked out the sun. While the roc slept, Sindbad ▶

Sindbad and his men set up camp on a sandy island and lit a fire. Suddenly, they discovered that the island was really a giant whale, which tipped them over into the sea, so that they had to swim for their lives.

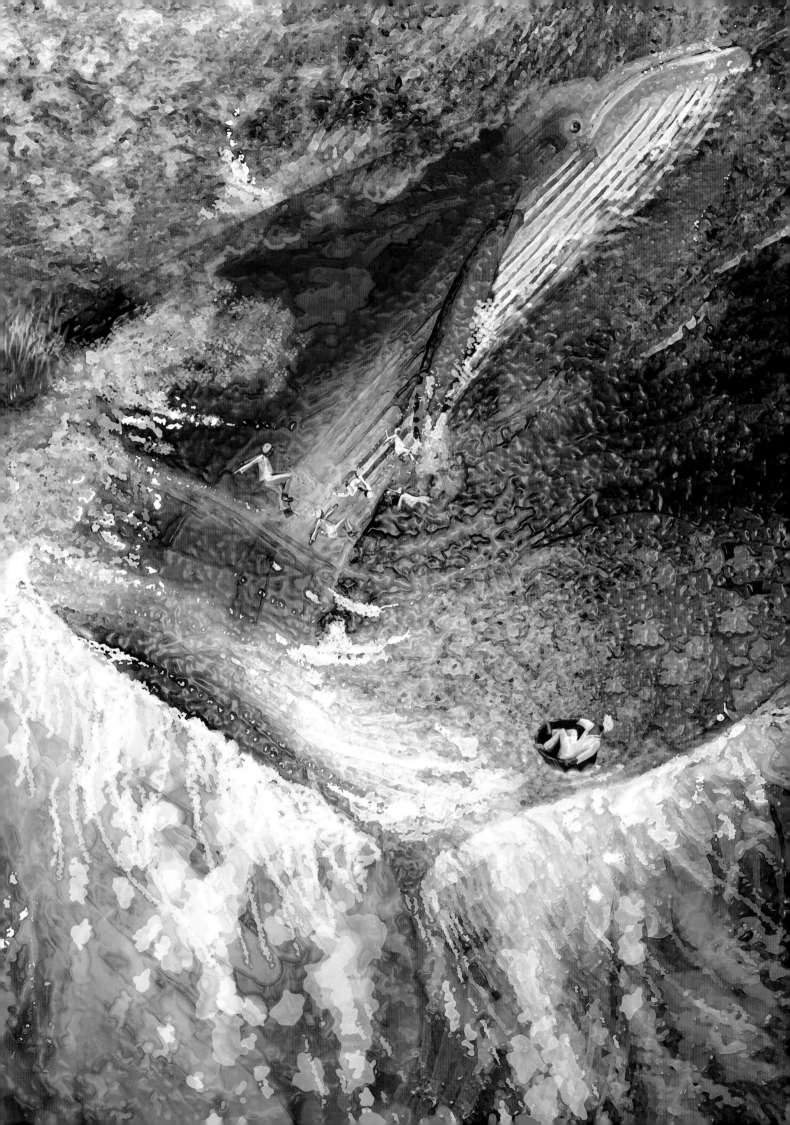

The Seven Voyages of Sindbad

unrolled the strip of cloth that made up the turban that was wound around his head. He carefully tied the cloth to the bird's huge claw. When the roc awoke from its sleep and beat its wings, Sindbad was abruptly transported far away from the island, clinging desperately to the roc.

At long last, the gigantic bird landed in a steep-sided valley, which was strewn from side to side with sparkling diamonds. Visiting traders used to get the diamonds by hurling legs of lamb into this valley. The precious stones would stick to the raw meat, which the greedy roc always carried back to its nest. Then the traders would scare the roc away and seize the precious diamonds.

Sindbad grabbed as many diamonds as he could, and then he clung onto a leg of lamb. Soon he was whisked away to the nest of the roc, diamonds and all. He was rescued from there by the traders, and he sailed home with a hold full of precious, glittering stones.

CONNECTIONS
• The cities of Baghdad and Basrah are in modern Iraq. At the time that the legend of Sindbad the Sailor was born, the two cities were at their most powerful.
• Haroun al-Raschid was a wise and learned man who ruled Arabia from about A.D. 785 to 809.
• Arab seafarers traveled far and wide across the Indian Ocean for more than a thousand years. Their wooden ships were called dhows and had huge triangular sails.
• Giant birds really did exist on Indian Ocean islands, although they couldn't fly. The elephant bird of Madagascar was 10 feet tall and weighed over 1,100 pounds. It had huge claws, massive legs, and a spearlike beak.

Seafarers and traders like Sindbad used boats called dhows to trade goods from Arabia to Madagascar, an island off the coast of Africa.

On his fifth voyage, Sindbad met the Old Man of the Sea, who asked him to carry him over a stream. Once he was on Sindbad's back, the old man refused to budge and tried to make him a slave.

Other adventures

On his many travels, Sindbad met rhinoceroses as tall as camels, which could impale elephants on their long, spiked noses. He saw huge fish the size of houses.

On his third voyage, Sindbad's ship was stolen by savage apes, and he fought a terrifying battle with a tree-sized ogre. It had long fangs and claws, and ate human flesh. He once encountered a snake, too, which swallowed up his friend in one gulp, cracking his bones like twigs. On his fourth voyage, Sindbad's crew were fattened up for the cooking pot by cannibals. Sick with grief, Sindbad escaped to a more friendly kingdom. He taught the horsemen there the craft of making saddles and stirrups, which they had never learned. He was richly rewarded for his work and married a noble lady. Sindbad loved her well, and although he missed his home in Baghdad, he lived there happily for a time.

Now in this kingdom, there was a strange and terrible custom. When a woman died, her husband was buried alive in her tomb. So when Sindbad's wife died of a fever, he was lowered into the death pit with her body. This foul underground cavern was piled high with corpses and skeletons. Days later, Sindbad found a route of escape, a burrow made by scavenging animals. At last he crawled to freedom, and was rescued from the shore where he found himself by a passing ship.

The land of coconuts

Surely Sindbad would never leave the safety of his home again? It is a strange fact that travelers often forget the past hardships they have suffered. One day on the wharf at Basrah, Sindbad saw a fine new ship and smelled the salt sea. He resolved to set sail on a fifth voyage and wander the world once more.

His crew were experienced sailors, but unlike Sindbad they had never come across a roc before. They sailed to an island where they smashed the huge egg of this giant bird, despite Sindbad's warnings. The terrible birds followed their ship out to sea and bombed it with massive rocks, which splintered the rudder and holed the stern. The vessel went spinning down to the bottom of the ocean. Sindbad, Allah be praised, was saved from drowning, and he was washed up on the shore of an island.

There he met the Old Man of the Sea, who asked Sindbad to carry him on his shoulders over a stream. Once he was on Sindbad's back, the old fellow locked his legs like a vise and would not move. He used Sindbad as a slave and beast of burden. But Sindbad was a cunning man. He made some wine in a gourd. The old man drank so much that he fell off his perch, and Sindbad killed him there and then. Later on that voyage,

Sindbad and his men threw pebbles at the monkeys in the palm trees, so that the monkeys would throw coconuts down on them.

Sindbad joined a group of people on an expedition to a coconut grove, where the palm trees were much too tall to climb. The people picked up pebbles and threw them at the monkeys that lived in the trees. The angry monkeys pelted the people with the coconuts! Sindbad collected many coconuts, and traded them for spices and pearls. He came home a wealthy man.

The true believer

On Sindbad's sixth voyage, he was shipwrecked on an island and befriended by the king, who sent him back to Baghdad with gifts for Haroun al-Raschid himself. On his seventh voyage, he lived in a land where the men grew wings, and he was carried high above the summit of a mountain. Sindbad praised Allah, and at once he was dropped like a stone. Sindbad realized he was not in a land of true believers. It was time to return to Baghdad. Ever after, Sindbad stayed home and never sailed again. He told his tales and the storytellers still tell them, from the Arabian Sea to the China Sea and the shores of Africa.

The Monkey and the Monk

The Journey to the West, or Xiyuji, is a cheerful mixture of fables, fairy tales, legends, and religious beliefs. They were collected by the Chinese poet, Wu Chengen, who lived in the 1500s, and were performed on stage.

There was trouble in China. The people there were falling into wicked ways. Up in heaven, the Buddha decided to do something about it. He summoned one of his saints, the merciful Guanyin. "Seek out one man who is a true believer," she was ordered. "Send him to India, to the Temple of the Thunder Clap, where our holiest scriptures are stored, to bring them back to China."

Monkey was a very bold creature who performed magical feats.

Guanyin traveled to the great city of Chang'an, where she searched high and low for a man who would bring the scriptures back to China, to show people the error of their ways. At last, she found the ideal man to send. He was a humble and wise monk. His name was Xuanzang, but he was known in the monastery as Brother Tripitaka. He was sent off by the emperor himself with these words: "Tripitaka, the journey ahead of you is very long and full of dangers. It will take many years, but if you succeed, you will save all the people in our land."

Meeting Monkey

Monks travel with no possessions other than a wooden staff and a simple bowl for begging alms. Guanyin decided to keep an eye over Tripitaka from heaven, but she soon realized that the monk would need some sturdy traveling companions to protect him.

The first companion she appointed was called Monkey. He was a bold, cheeky fellow, if ever there was one. For hundreds of years, Monkey had been learning all kinds of magical tricks. He could somersault into the air and even change shape. He often battled against monsters, spirits, dragons, and demons, and always sent them away. Monkey had even soared up into heaven itself, where he created all kinds of mischief. The Buddha himself had had to take Monkey in hand, imprisoning him in a stone chest for 500 years, deep under a mountain. When Tripitaka came to this mountain, Monkey was given a chance to make good. He burst out from his mountain prison, boasting and bellowing and banging his chest. Guanyin realized that Monkey might become mischievous, so she gave Tripitaka a spell that would bring him to heel if necessary.

Monkey soon proved his worth. One day, when they were attacked by a snarling tiger, he drew an embroidery needle from behind his ear. It immediately grew into a big iron cudgel, which Monkey brought crashing down on the beast's head. Tripitaka was taken aback.

"Come on, a tiger skin will help to keep us warm next winter," Monkey laughed.

Winter came all too soon. Snow weighed down the branches of the trees, and icicles hung from the cliffs and gorges they passed. At Eagle Grief Stream, a hungry dragon gobbled up Tripitaka's horse, so Guanyin herself turned the dragon into a magic steed, to carry the monk forward along the stony road. The snow melted with the coming of spring. Blossom covered the orchards.

At one small farm, they found a family being terrorized by a pig-monster. He had a long snout and was nicknamed "Greedy Pig." Monkey tricked him by pretending to be the farmer's daughter. When Greedy Pig revealed that he had once served as a general up in heaven, Monkey forced him to join them on their journey. Guanyin approved, for the pig's military training skills proved useful. The pig did mend his loutish ways, but he always remained a bit quarrelsome.

Sandy of the river

Summer turned to misty fall before they met the third companion at the River of Floating Sands. "Sandy" was a water monster, with nine human skulls rattling on a necklace around his neck, and eyes like glowing lanterns. Greedy Pig and Monkey fought him for days on end, but they could not beat him. Finally, they had to go up to heaven and ask Guanyin for help.

"Idiots," she laughed at them. "I put Sandy there myself, to guard the river. You only need to tell him you're working for me." So Sandy, too, became a pilgrim. He never stopped grumbling, though.

A magic spell turned Sandy's gruesome necklace into a boat, so they could all cross the river. What a disreputable crew they made! But their weaknesses and failings only made Tripitaka more determined to find the scriptures. Perhaps even these misfits would find holiness one day.

To foil a ghost king, Monkey flew up to heaven on a cloud to consult the wise Laozi.

The seasons came around again and again, and the years passed. The monk and his followers traveled far, through stony wilderness and lush valleys, over muddy plains and lakeshores. Soon, their passport was stamped with the seals of many distant kingdoms. Although Tripitaka dreamed of reaching the temple in distant India, his companions only thought of their day-to-day adventures.

Monkey to the rescue

In one land, Tripitaka met the ghost of a king. His throne had been seized by a magician, who had taken on the real king's appearance and thrown him down a well. Monkey soon fixed that situation. He flew up to heaven on a cloud, and paid a visit to the wise old master, Laozi.

"Give me a thousand of your pills for bringing people back to life!" demanded Monkey.

"Trust you to demand more than your fair share," exclaimed Laozi, who knew Monkey of old. "Here, one is quite enough for you!"

With this, they brought the king back to life, and after Monkey had chased the magician halfway across the sky, the true king was restored to his throne and family.

Continuing their journey, in the next country they reached, the travelers found that honest Buddhists ▶

The Monkey and the Monk

Monkey summoned up fiery dragons in the clouds to impress the king.

were being treated with great injustice by the king. He had fallen under the influence of some wizards who were pretending to be Taoist priests. They challenged our travelers to a contest of wizardry, to prove that no Buddhists could compete with their own magical powers. But again, Monkey rose to the occasion.

While the wizards chanted rainmaking spells in vain, Monkey spoke with the gods and made water cascade down from the sky. He then called up dragons to stage a fiery spectacle in the clouds. For another test, fifty tables were piled on top of each other to make a tower. Tripitaka flew to the top and stayed still. But, when one of the wizards tried it, a spell from Monkey made his head itch with lice. He scratched, wobbled slightly, and fell.

Monkey used sly tricks to win all the guessing games and then demanded an execution contest. Their heads were chopped off—but Monkey's grew back on his shoulders again! Finally, the competition was clinched when Monkey jumped into a cauldron of boiling oil, an event which he alone survived. Greatly impressed, the king of that land became a Buddhist, and wished Tripitaka and the pilgrims a safe and successful journey.

Breaking the ice

Sometimes Tripitaka thought he would never reach India, but onward he rode, with the tricky trio striding along beside him. One starlit night, they came to a great body of shining water called the River that Leads to Heaven. It

was as wide as an ocean. While they were wondering what to do next, they heard music from a nearby village and went to speak to the people there.

It seemed that the local king was a monster from the great river, who was demanding the villagers' children to eat. Monkey would not stand that for a moment. He changed himself into a young boy, and Greedy Pig changed himself into a little girl.

The villagers gave these two "children" to the monster, who was already licking his lips with delight. In a flash, the pilgrims returned to their own true shapes, and then gave the beast such a savage beating that he rushed back to his home under the great river.

In revenge, the monster-king had the river frozen over. Tripitaka ventured out on the ice, eager to continue his journey. Alas, the ice broke and the monk fell into the river. The monster-king locked him up inside a stone chest in his underwater palace. Who else could rescue him, but our brave heroes?

CONNECTIONS

• The character of Brother Tripitaka, the monk in this tale, is based on a historical figure. The real Xuanzang, or Tripitaka, lived from A.D. 602–664, and he traveled to India from China between 631 and 635.

• China has three main religious traditions. These are the Taoist religion, which was founded by Laozi in the 500s B.C., the teachings of Kongfuzi, or Confucius (551–497 B.C.), and the Buddhist religion, which entered China from India. The latter religion was founded by the Buddha (Gautama Siddhartha), who lived from about 563 to 483 B.C.

• For a time there was rivalry between Taoism and Buddhism in China, but over the ages, all three beliefs became intertwined and mixed up with belief in spirits, demons, and magic.

• In the lifetime of Xuanzang, Chang'an was the capital of China. Today it is the large city of Xi'an.

The Buddha preached that all earthly desires lead to suffering, and that rejection of them is the only way to happiness. Xuanzang (Tripitaka) clearly led a holy life, but his traveling companions showed passion, violence, greed, and many other common faults. The writer of the tale smiled at their weaknesses and in the end, gave them their reward in heaven, too.

Temples and spirits

Back on shore again, the four pilgrims faced a long wait. At last, warmer weather came. The river melted and the pilgrims crossed over, riding on the back of a giant turtle. After many more months, they came to a warm and sunny land, where fiery flowers glowed like gems, and the people were pious and holy.

"So this is India," exclaimed Tripitaka. "Our journey is almost complete!" His weatherbeaten, wrinkled face was wreathed in beaming smiles. Monkey capered around and Greedy Pig snorted. Sandy looked at their dusty clothes. "We all need to wash," he said, wearily looking at their grim faces, "and a drink of cool, fresh water." Soon they came to a river, by the Jade Truth Temple at the foot of the Holy Mountain. They cleaned themselves up, but now they had to get across. It was very rough and the ferryman's boat had no bottom! Even so, they climbed aboard and were astonished to see Tripitaka's body float across the water. He did not drown. He was now a spirit and had no further need for a mortal body.

At the summit of the mountain, they finally reached their goal. The Buddha himself appeared before the transformed monk and his traveling companions. His words echoed around the peaks like chiming bells: "Welcome to the Temple of the Thunder Clap, my faithful pilgrims! The Holy Scriptures are here for your collection." His smile shone like the sun.

Return and reward

The return journey was swift, for Tripitaka and our intrepid heroes were aided on their way by heavenly winds. They came at last to Chang'an after fourteen years of absence, and there they presented the Chinese emperor with 5,048 sacred scrolls. A great banquet was held in their honor at the palace.

Then they were carried away to the realms of heaven. Tripitaka was made an Enlightened One, and his horse was turned into one of the eight most senior Heavenly Dragons.

The three others, too, were given special awards for their holiness. Even then, Monkey, Greedy Pig, and Sandy never stopped grumbling and fooling around.

Heaven would never be very peaceful with them around. Tripitaka sighed and smiled a contented smile.

At the end of their long journey from China, the Buddha welcomed Monkey and the spirit form of Tripitaka to the Temple of the Thunder Clap.

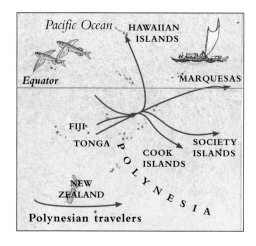

Kupe the Explorer

The Polynesians, whose ancestors originated in Southeast Asia, settled the Pacific islands from 1500 B.C. Like the legendary explorer, Kupe, they had no maps and steered by the stars. Their last great migration was southwest from the Society Islands (French Polynesia)—they reached New Zealand in the A.D. 900s. Their descendants are the Maoris.

There are as many stories as there are fish in the sea, said the teller of tales. Have you heard of faraway Hawaiki, the island of the rising sun? They say that the sweet potato grows there without having to be planted. The bubbling waters around Hawaiki teem with fish. That is where the cuckoo flies during the cold months of winter. Many brave warriors have followed the cuckoo back again in spring, sailing to our land from Hawaiki in a fleet of great, ocean-going canoes.

Kupe was the first of these explorers, the greatest chief ever to go to sea, hunter of the giant octopus, shaper of the lands, and commander of many canoes. With him came his family and other members of his clan. The brave chief Ngake, Kupe's closest friend, brought his people, too. Skimming across the green waves one day, Kupe and his wife Hine-te-apa-rangi spied a range of cloud-covered hills on the horizon. The crew dug their paddles into the water and drew alongside the mass of land.

The shining cuckoo flew from Hawaiki.

Rocks and surf

Kupe leaped ashore, but the ground was pitching and tossing like some great log. He had to anchor it with heavy stones until it held fast. That day, Kupe became the first man ever to set foot on Aotearoa, Land of the Long White Cloud. Kupe explored this new land. He discovered forests, bubbling mud pools, and water that gushed up from the ground like the spouting of a whale at sea. Kupe paddled around capes, coves, and beaches. With a stroke of his mighty paddle, Kupe cut Aotearoa into two islands and sailed through the strait that opened up before him. He explored the western coast of the northern island, braving the high ocean swell and the crashing surf.

We know the route of Kupe's voyage, for he left many of his possessions on the way—the triangular sails of his canoe, his bailer, fishing nets, and dogs. These all survived because they were turned to stone, forming boulders and

CONNECTIONS

• Hawaiki was a mythical island in the eastern Pacific, where humans were first created by the god Tane. It was believed to be the homeland of the Maori people, and may have been one of the Society Islands.

• Kupe may have been based on one or more of the chiefs who settled in New Zealand over 1,000 years ago. It is said he could do magic, and control the waves and the forests.

• Aotearoa is the North Island of New Zealand, and Hokianga harbor lies in the far northwest. Te-whanga-nui-a-Tara is now Wellington harbor.

A land of snowy peaks and grassy meadows greeted the first Polynesian voyagers. This is Mount Cook on South Island.

cliffs around the coast. Using these landmarks, later seafarers could navigate the coast of Aotearoa with ease. There is a boulder that marks safe passage into the harbor at Porirua. This was once the anchor stone of Kupe's canoe, but he exchanged it for a new one. The small rocky islands in Te-whanga-nui-a-Tara carry the names of Kupe's daughters, Matiu and Makaro. There are records of Kupe's voyage everywhere.

The southern voyage

Kupe and his trusted companion Ngake led his fleet of canoes onward. He now turned south again to follow the coast of the other great island he had cut free from Aotearoa. This was a good land with rich, black soil and valuable stone. It had snow-capped mountains and frozen rivers of ice.

In the far south, Ngake's wife, Hine-waihua, left behind some of her pets, including seals and penguins. The descendants of those creatures still live there today. Whenever the canoes were hauled up on some lonely shore, they were never met by fierce warriors and war chants. There were no smoking camp fires. There was nothing but the clamor of birds and the whistling of the wind. No one lived on these islands.

Return to Hawaiki

Kupe, however, was not the one to settle here himself. Longing to return to Hawaiki, he sailed back to the far north of Aotearoa. There he held a farewell feast. One day, Kupe and his wife raised anchor in Hokianga harbor, and steered an eastward course toward the rising sun. They voyaged safely to Hawaiki, and never returned to Aotearoa again. However, their children and their children's children arrived here in their fleets of canoes, with sweet potatoes and seeds, and weapons for hunting. The islands were theirs for the taking.

Kupe and Ngake sailed their canoes through the islands, leaving landmarks for future seafarers.

AUSTRALIA

New South Wales

Lithgow

Wombeyan

Jenolan Caves

Goulburn

Tasman Sea

The One That Got Away

This tale is from the Gundungurra, an Aboriginal people from the Blue Mountains of New South Wales, Australia. The blue haze of the highlands is a trick of the light, which is caused by evaporating oil from the eucalyptus trees. Ancient tales tell how this beautiful landscape was shaped long ago, in the "Dreamtime," when magical animal-humans lived on Earth.

Like all fishermen, Mirrigan the Tiger-cat was a dreamer. He longed to catch a really enormous fish, not the little minnows and eels he trapped every day in the billabongs and creeks where he hunted. So one fine morning, Mirrigan picked up his dillybag, and set out with his spears and nets. He traveled along streams, until at last he came to a place where two rivers joined together—the Wollondilly and the Wingeecaribbee.

Mirrigan waded out to a sandbank and stood stock-still, his fishing spear raised. Through the shimmering water, he thought he saw the glint of a huge eye. He hurled his spear into the depths. There was a great swelling of the waters—and then nothing but ripples.

Only one creature was big enough to make such a commotion. It was Gurrangatch, a monster that was half lizard, half fish. Mirrigan had heard rumors of this creature's fearsome powers, but he was not afraid. He was sure he could outwit the old rogue. He stripped a special bark called millewa from nearby trees and dropped it in

the river. The bark was poisonous, and soon it was clouding the water. Deep in his lair, Gurrangatch suddenly felt drowsy and sick, but realized just in time what was happening. With one great convulsion, he shot to the surface. His massive tail smashed the water, throwing up a curtain of spray in the sunlight. Gurrangatch then tore off through solid earth and rock, as if it was nothing more than water and weed. Behind him rolled a wall of water, which created new rivers and underground streams. He thrashed this way and that, looping back to the banks of the Wollondilly and away.

The big chase

Mirrigan, who had been busy collecting more poisonous bark, returned to find that Gurrangatch had fled. In a rage, he ran along the banks of the new rivers, mile after mile, catching only distant glimpses of the angry monster. At last, Mirrigan caught up with his prey at Wombeyan. Mirrigan tried to poke him with a pole.

CONNECTIONS

• The traditional home of the Gundungurra stretched from what is now Lithgow in the Blue Mountains, eastward to the Nepean river and southward to Goulburn.

• Aboriginal tales of ancient history, or Dreamtime, tell how their ancestors were both animal and human, and created the landscape and environment in which we live.

• The idea that mountains and rivers were created long ago by gods, human ancestors, or mythical beasts, is found in many cultures. In a Maori story, the natural features of New Zealand are explained by the travels of Kupe the Explorer.

Many legends portray people as animals. The four Diving-bird men came to help Mirrigan the Tiger-cat as he tried to capture Gurrangatch.

"Will this meddlesome Tiger-cat never stop pestering me?" grumbled and gurgled Gurrangatch.

So he set off across the land once more, with Mirrigan the Tiger-cat in hot pursuit. One day the chase led back past Mirrigan's own home, and his family had to race up the hillside to keep from being drowned. "Where have you been all this time, you fool?" yelled Mirrigan's furious wife, seeing the demented hunter. "This monster is destroying the whole of our land!"

"I can't stop!" panted Mirrigan as he raced by. "I just have to catch him!"

And so they continued. One day Gurrangatch was cornered on some slippery rocks. The two enemies traded blows, wooden club against the lashing, scaly tail. The riverbed shook for miles downstream. But Gurrangatch escaped again, this time to Katoomba.

Finally, at the Jenolan caves, Mirrigan built a huge wall to hem the monster in. But who on earth could raise Gurrangatch from the depths? Suddenly, Mirrigan remembered some friends of his. He set off westward, and after many days, he found them at their hunting camp. They were Wood Duck, Black Duck, Shag, and Diver.

When Mirrigan the Tiger-cat tried to capture Gurrangatch, the monster thrashed his huge tail and created a wall of water that swept through the land.

"Come with me, fellows," he shouted to the Diving-bird men. Alas, it was still hopeless. Shoals of fish tried to hide Gurrangatch from view, and the giant lizard-fish sank down deeper and deeper. All four diving-birds tried to haul him back up, but he was too heavy for them. All that came up in their beaks was a piece of fin and shiny scales.

The dream

As Mirrigan peered at this catch, he caught sight of his reflection in the water. Who was this gaunt, scarred figure? How long had he been chasing the monster? Weeks? Months? Years? Weariness took hold of him. He fell asleep and dreamed.

Mirrigan dreamed of his family, of his children's children, and the age of men. He dreamed that the streams, water holes, billabongs, and rivers carved out by Gurrangatch flowed onward into the silver future. And he dreamed that the spirit of Gurrangatch would lie deep in these waters, guarding them for all time.

When he awoke at last, a beautiful dawn lit up the Blue Mountains. He picked up his dillybag, nodded at the Diving-bird men, and set off for home.

Glossary

aborigines The first people to live in a land, the original inhabitants. The term "Aborigine" is used especially to describe the first Australians.

Aeneas A Trojan whom the ancient Romans claimed as their ancestor.

ancestors Long-dead members of a family, such as great-great-grandparents, from whom generations that are living are descended.

Arthur A legendary leader of the British Celts in their wars against invading Saxons in the sixth century A.D. In later medieval times he was portrayed as a great Christian king, and he appears in literature across Western Europe.

Asgard In Norse mythology, the land of the gods. It was linked to Midgard by a rainbow bridge.

Aso In West African tales, Aso was the wife of Kwaku Ananse, the spider-man, who planned how he was to fulfill his quest.

Aztecs Native American people who lived in Northern and Central Mexico. The empire they built up was at its most powerful from A.D. 1350 to 1520.

Bible The holy book of the Jewish and Christian faiths.

Buddha The Enlightened One, the name given to Gautama Siddhartha (c563–483 B.C.), who founded the Buddhist faith.

Buddhism A religion that teaches that suffering is caused by material desire and that humans are reborn many times.

Calypso A Greek nymph who healed and enchanted Odysseus.

Camelot In Arthurian legend, King Arthur's castle and the seat of the Knights of the Round Table.

Circe In Greek mythology, an enchantress who changed Odysseus' crew into pigs.

civilization A society that has a settled population, towns and cities, laws, education, arts, crafts, and sciences.

cosmos The ordered whole of Earth and the heavens.

culture A collective word for the beliefs, customs, language, and way of life that identify a particular people or civilization.

Cyclopes The race of one-eyed, man-eating giants that were encountered by both Odysseus and Aeneas.

deity God or goddess.

Dido A Phoenician queen who built the city of Carthage (near modern Tunis in North Africa) and fell in love with Aeneas.

divine Sacred or like a god.

Dreamtime The continuing state of creation and being that is central to the beliefs of the Australian Aborigines.

Elen Daughter of Eudaf in the Welsh tales. Emperor Macsen dreams of and marries her.

Enkidu A wild man, fashioned from clay by the goddess, Aruru, in order to challenge the growing power of the king, the mighty Gilgamesh.

eternity Time without end, forever.

Etzel (Attila) King of the Huns, whom Kriemhild married to wreak revenge on her treacherous knights and brothers.

Fionn Mac Cumhail The superhuman father of the Irish hero, Oisin, and leader of the Fianna, a band of warriors.

Galahad The name of several characters in Arthurian legends. In some stories he is the son of Lancelot. As the purest knight, he completes the quest for the Holy Grail.

Gilgamesh A legendary hero of the Sumerians, Gilgamesh was the king of the great city of Uruk (in modern Iraq) and the friend of Enkidu, the wild man.

Guanyin The Chinese goddess of mercy. She recruited Tripitaka and Monkey to fetch the Buddhist scrolls from India and bring them back to China.

Guinevere In Arthurian legends, the wife of King Arthur and the lover of Sir Lancelot.

Hades In Greek mythology, Hades was ruler of the dead. The name was later used to describe his kingdom.

Hagen The grim Burgundian knight who had Siegfried killed.

Harpies The "snatchers" of Greek mythology—fearsome hags with the faces of women and the wings and claws of birds.

Holy Grail A mystical chalice, or cup, sought by King Arthur and his knights.

Huitzilopochtli The Aztec god of the sun and war, who led the Mexica's migration from their homeland. He may have been a mortal chief, who was made into a god when he died.

Knights of the Round Table King Arthur's knights, who undertook the search for the Holy Grail.

Kriemhild The beautiful princess of Burgundy, who loved Siegfried and sought revenge after his death.

Kupe The legendary Maori chief who discovered New Zealand.

Kwaku Ananse The spider-man storyteller and trickster of West African folk tales.

Lancelot King Arthur's most trusted knight, who falls in love with Arthur's wife Queen Guinevere.

Laozi The wise old master who helped Monkey and his friends. Founder of the Taoist faith in China.

legend An old story that has been handed down over the years. It is often rooted in historical figures or events.

Loki In Norse mythology, Loki was a handsome devil, a trickster who could change shape into other creatures.

Mabinogion A series of tales written down in Wales in the Middle Ages, based on ancient Celtic myths and legends.

Macsen The Roman leader of the Britons from the Mabinogion stories.

Mexica A name used by the Aztec people when they migrated to find a new home.

Midgard In Norse mythology, the land of men and women. It was linked to Asgard by a rainbow bridge.

migration Movement of people (or animals or birds) from one region to settle in another, either permanently, or at certain times of the year.

Monkey A bold, cheeky creature who is the hero of the Chinese tale *Journey to the West* and who helped Tripitaka bring the Buddhist scriptures back to China.

Morning Star A Native American god who brought Scarface up to Sun, his father, who healed him.

myth A story with supernatural beings such as spirits, gods, and monsters, which has been handed down through generations. Myths usually reflect the beliefs and customs of a society.

mythology The collected myths and beliefs of a society.

Niamh Beautiful maiden who leads Oisin to the fairy kingdom of Tir na nÓg.

Odysseus A Greek hero who was prevented by the gods from returning home after the Trojan wars. He went on many long adventures.

Oisin An Irish hero who journeyed to the fairy kingdom of Tir na nÓg.

Old Man of the Sea Used Sindbad as a slave and beast of burden.

Olympian One of 12 Greek gods who lived on Mount Olympus and involved themselves in the affairs of humans.

Olympus The sacred mountain in Northern Greece that was believed to be the home of the gods.

Poseidon In Greek mythology, Lord and Ruler of the Sea and enemy of Odysseus.

ritual A series of actions or ceremonies, often performed as part of worship or making offerings to the gods.

Sandy A water monster with nine human skulls rattling on a necklace around his neck. He was a river guard appointed by Guanyin, the Chinese goddess.

Scarface In North American mythology, this is the disfigured human who is carried up to the sky. He returns with a gift from the gods—the first sweat lodge.

Shahrazad For 1,001 nights, she stayed alive by telling her tales to the king, such as the story of Sindbad the Sailor.

Siegfried The superhero and ruler of the Netherlands and Norway, also conqueror of the Nibelungs. He marries Kriemhild, Princess of Burgundy, and he is killed by her brothers.

Sindbad The Arab sailor who made seven perilous voyages.

Sirens In Greek mythology, these creatures were birds with the faces of beautiful women, who lured sailors to their death with their singing.

sun One of the five worlds that the Aztecs believed was created and then destroyed.

Sun In Native American legend, the sun god who healed Scarface with his heat and taught him to use the sweat lodge to cure his people's ills back on Earth. He is the father of Morning Star.

Taoism The ancient Chinese belief in spirits and natural harmony, which later became a complex religion with gods and goddesses. Tao means "the way."

Tenochtitlán The historic capital city of the Mexica or Aztec people, built on the site of modern Mexico City.

Thor In Norse mythology, the god of war, thunder, and storms. He carries a hammer and is an enemy of the Giants.

Tir na nÓg In Celtic mythology, the Land of Eternal Youth, across the western ocean.

tradition Habits, customs, and beliefs handed down through generations to become part of a people's identity.

tribe A group of people who share a common language, often led by a chief.

Tripitaka A Chinese Buddhist, born as Xuanzang in A.D. 602. His adventures with Monkey, bringing the Buddhist scrolls back to China, are told in the epic story of the *Journey to the West*.

Trojans Wandering peoples from the conquered city of Troy who became ancestors of the Romans.

Troy An ancient city in what is now Western Turkey, home of the Trojans. It was attacked by the Greeks over 3,000 years ago.

Utgard In Viking mythology, the home of a race of Giants who were enemies of the gods and goddesses.

Utgardaloki A giant king who challenges Thor and his companions in Scandinavian legend.

Utnapishtim The gods grant him the gift of eternal life in the Gilgamesh epic.

Venus The Roman goddess of love and beauty, said to be the mother of Aeneas. She is the Greek goddess Aphrodite.

Zeus The chief Olympian god in the mythology of ancient Greece. He was known to the Romans as Jupiter or Jove.

Index